CULTURE CLASH

ELLEN MATTHEWS

CULTURE CLASH

INTERCULTURAL PRESS INC. CHICAGO

To Ben...

who held us all together.

Published by:

Intercultural Press, Inc.
70 W. Hubbard Street
Chicago, IL 60610
(312) 321-0075

ISBN: 0-933662-48-3

Library of Congress No.: 81-85714

Printed in the U.S.A.

INTRODUCTION

The events in this book take place between August, 1975, shortly after Kim and Quang arrived in this country as Vietnamese refugees, and mid-1979, by which time we had gone from being their sponsors to sometime counselors and lasting friends. In a sense this is also the story of the sponsorship program, without which we would never have known them at all...the story of our personal strengths and weaknesses and those of the program, which continues to exist today.

Between April 25 and May 1, 1975, nearly 100,000 South Vietnamese fled their country for the United States during the communist takeover of Saigon. Although they continued to leave in smaller numbers after that, this large initial outpouring set the mechanics of the sponsorship program in motion. A refugee center was hastily set up in Guam, and several aging military bases were reactivated in this country to serve as temporary resettlement camps. The major task would be to move the refugees out of the camps and into American society as quickly and painlessly (from a federal point of view) as possible. The theory was that if each family went out under the aegis of a private American sponsor, then they could be quietly scattered across the country and assimilated.

Although a federal Interagency Task Force for Indochina Refugees was established to administer the resettlement, the real work was done by a group of voluntary agencies—Catholic Charities and Lutheran Social Services among others—which had access to large numbers of potential sponsors through their church networks. A sponsor would take a refugee family in, provide temporary shelter, and see to finding jobs, medical aid, schooling—whatever was necessary to get the family on the road to independence. Some voluntary agencies allowed the sponsors to request $300 for each refugee; others kept this federal money for administrative expenses. At any rate, the sponsor had no legal obligation to support the refugees, only a moral one.

123507

Given this tentative nature of the arrangement, an ideal sponsor, from a voluntary agency's point of view, was a church. A church could raise enough money, organize enough man-and woman power and exert enough influence to resettle the large extended families common among the refugees...or so the theory went. Moreover, the church structure itself guaranteed a kind of built-in conscience. The refugees were unlikely to be mistreated.

But because there were so many refugees in that initial outpouring, the agencies also had to consider individual families, like ours, as sponsors. Kim and Quang came to us through our personal request, an interview with a Catholic Charities representative and a computer, which matched Quang's job skills with Ben's requirements for an employee. Not much basis for a new beginning, but there we were.

Except for our lack of church-affiliation, we were all fairly typical of the 1975 sponsors and refugees. Kim and Quang were in their 20's (many of the refugees were young), high-school educated and well-mannered. Although they were newlyweds, Kim's father had entrusted them with the care of Kim's two teenaged sisters—an almost unthinkable arrangement by American standards but not unusual by theirs. Ben and I were some ten years older, parents of three small children, owners of a small business where Quang would be able to work. Ben's Vietnamese military tour before our marriage gave him some background for our undertaking. I was staying at home with our preschoolers, doing some freelance writing, available to do the legwork we thought would be involved.

For the rest, I fall back on what one of the directors of Catholic Charities in Baltimore said to me recently as we rehashed all we had been through from the beginning. "In 1975," she told me, "none of us knew what we were doing."

In retrospect, this seems particularly apt. It hadn't occurred to anyone—certainly not to Ben and me—that the refugees would come to this country with a preconceived notion of life here quite different from what we understood to be the lot of refugees and immigrants. Even less did it occur to us that they would have preconceived ideas about what *our* role should be, as sponsors.

And so began what in this journal I've termed The Long First Year, when we found ourselves offering what we thought was help but what Kim and Quang seemed to regard as a kind of torture. For the first six months we battled not only Kim and Quang's expectations—of gifts, of services, of patronage we had never intended to provide—but also our own doubts and the criticism of the churches in our community, which were providing other refugee families many more goods and favors than Kim and Quang were getting from us. By the spring of 1976, everything had equalized. The churches had taken longer to go through the process we had travelled, but now they caught up with us, and the phases were the same. The initial surge of sympathy had tapered off into a desire for the refugees to become more independent. The refugees, bewildered, clung to their support systems frantically...much to the annoyance of the sponsors. The sponsors hardened their positions: it was to be self-support or nothing. And finally there was resolution, not always happy. The spring of 1976 was the beginning of the mass wave of secondary migration...from wherever the refugees had been sent first by the government, to wherever they wanted to be, usually California or Texas, near their peers.

Looking back, it is easier than it was then to see why so much bitterness and confusion surfaced that first year. It's easier to admit the cruelty we sponsors inflicted on the refugees, through misunderstanding rather than malice. But in 1975 we were mired in it, and it was hard to make sense of anything. None of us had anticipated how helpless we would be in the face of our cultural differences. Words meant one thing to Americans and something else to the Vietnamese, translations aside. There seemed to be no getting across, partly because there was no one to help us who had lived on both sides of the bridge. It was "Us" against "Them," where our intent had been conciliation.

For ourselves, Ben and I relied on his memory of Vietnam as it had been in 1968, when he had worked with Vietnamese ARVN units not far from the village where Quang was born. The picture of the culture we managed to piece together was crude, but it lent a semblance of reason to what was happening. Many sponsors didn't have even that. In the spring, Kim and Quang were among the few refugees to stay...not because they were so delighted with us, or with Maryland, but because their personal circumstances made it easier not to travel. And so we had the opportunity to watch them heal.

Over the next few years they changed enormously. The second, shorter part of this journal is primarily about how they learned to deal with our work ethic, which is quite different from their own system of patronage. Many other things happened that are not told here. The past few years have seen a struggle within the family between American ways and Vietnamese ones. Kim, particularly, has fought against too much assimilation. When Lan, her sister, found a Vietnamese boyfriend in her senior year of high school and threatened to run off to California to marry him after graduation, a great battle of wits ensued. Kim's father had entrusted Lan to her; he wanted her to keep the family together. In a way almost incomprehensible to an American mind, Kim fought not to break that trust. And in many other ways, so subtle that they are difficult to define, we remain products of very different backgounds.

Even when we think the meanings of surface actions seem perfectly obvious, they often aren't. One incident in particular always reminds me of this. By October 1979, Kim's family had come full circle and were themselves sponsoring a refugee family, a distant uncle of hers who escaped Vietnam in a fishing boat with his wife and three children. A reporter soon came to interview the uncle, with Minh, Kim's youngest sister, acting as interpreter. At the end of the interview, Minh—a high schol senior then—began to reminisce about her own first impressions of America four years earlier.

"When I first meet Ben and Ellen," she said, "I really scare. I never was around any Americans before. I always stay with my family."

And this struck me as especially odd because my memory of that meeting was of Minh's extraordinary composure, the presence of mind which had allowed her, a 14-year-old, to cheerfully whisk our baby outside at the very moment he was becoming a nuisance. So it goes: much as we try to plumb each other's motives by reading outward actions, there remains an enormous margin of error. Our thought patterns have been cut on different cultural wheels, for which only some of the parts are the same. For six years we've been trying to analyze each other, and still there is the chance that any given conclusion is wrong—thrown hopelessly askew by some wrinkle of cultural background we have missed. This is a book about things as they have *seemed* to us, from our peculiarly American perspective. Our names and the name of our town have been changed in this account. Everything else is true.

Ellen Matthews
June 1981

PART ONE

THE LONG FIRST YEAR

ONE

I am beginning this journal because, in the two weeks since we first met them, the Vietnamese family has managed to overturn almost every preconception I had about them, so much so that now I seem to need a record to keep track. Even in the three days since they arrived at our house, nothing has been as I would have predicted...much more pleasant, in fact. We talk around our language barrier, share the house, go to the store—and they accept whatever we offer with such good cheer that we are amazed, prepared as we were for their reticence and unease. Strange food, stranger surroundings, nothing seems to phase them. They do not seem upset or nervous or even worried. Our time together—this serious-sounding business of sponsoring a refugee family—has been like a game.

But now, tonight, their lack of worry seems almost disturbing, out of synch with the flow of events. Quang has come down from the bedroom with a huge stack of records in his hand (mostly 45's)...with Minh, his sister-in-law, behind him, hands full of cassette tapes containing Vietnamese rock music. "I want to get...this," Quang says, patting our cassette player. And Ben, the good host, lends it to him in the meantime.

This, then, is the end of their unpacking. In those five cardboard boxes they brought with them were a few clothes, some snapshots of Kim's family at her father's house in Saigon...and hundreds of records and tapes. Pickings, it would seem, for a weekend outing rather than permanent flight from home.

And so now I sit in the bedroom writing, while the family remains downstairs listening to a woman singing in a high nasal twang, in a language I do not understand. I want to make sense of it. What possesses someone to leave a country forever, to take to the seas under the most urgent of circumstances, without gold, without survival items, carrying boxes of snapshots and tapes? Youth, perhaps? Even Quang, with his four years' experience in the Vietnamese Navy,

3

is only 25. Yet when I try to picture them packing for flight, the records seem absurd. I am reminded that our first meeting two weeks ago at the Indiantown Gap resettlement center caught me equally off guard. Kim and Quang have never been what I expected.

At that initial meeting, the family was sent to the recreation center after we'd been waiting for them for an hour, Ben and the baby and I. And my first thought was, no, this couldn't be. This attractive well-dressed family must be visitors, this glowing young woman and her husband, her two teenaged sisters at her side. Refugees were more rag-tag, weak with hunger, the shine gone from their eyes. My mind, floundering, made no adjustment to the fact that they'd been living at Indiantown Gap for a month then, and that their lives must have calmed down since their flight.

Kim, 20 years old and taller than I'd expected at 5'5", looked more like a model than the familiar newspaper pictures of haggard refugees. Dressed in a brown skirt and lime-colored sweater, long black hair held back from her face by a pearl barrette, doe-eyed and slender, she was as lovely as any Vietnamese I'd seen. Her eyes were accented with pale shadow, lips bright with gloss. And when I'd taken in her face, my gaze went quickly to her ring, a huge opal, obviously genuine, gleaming beneath long polished nails. Here was our refugee. Then she smiled and I, who should have been doing the reassuring, was reassured.

There was more: Lan, Kim's 16-year-old sister, long hair hanging sleek from her shoulders, neat in red polyester slacks and a tee shirt; Minh, the youngest sister, 14, shorter and chubbier but equally composed—two color plates from a Sears catalog. My first thought was: where did the clothes come from? Brought from Saigon? Unlikely. Donated? They seemed too stylish, too new. And two weeks later I still don't know. Perhaps acquired by the government and given out, along with immunization shots and Social Security cards. Or perhaps selected carefully from the belongings of all their friends, to strike just the right note for their new lives? Only their shoes were out of place—foam rubber shower shoes instead of real sandals. But still they were elegant enough, so that, standing there before us, Minha and Lan were able to reach out for our baby, Steve, with perfect assurance, as if they had known him from birth. Smiling, caressing his eyebrows, marvelling at the carroty color of his hair. "Oh-range," they said, and laughed as if his paleness itself were a source of delight.

Only Quang, shorter than Kim and wiry, a manila envelope of official papers clutched in his hand, was nervous, sweating slightly beneath a thin white dress shirt. We sat down at one of the picnic tables that lines the recreation hall and prepared to discuss terms, Quang with his papers spread out before him—immunization records, identification cards, Social Security numbers, Kim adjacent, long hair lifted slightly by the breeze from the fan, the girls at her side, Ben across. I stood behind Ben, jiggling Steve in my arms. Quang speaks a little English, Catholic Charities has told us. They have not told us *how* little. No matter, language is a small problem. Kim rises from the table, brings another young man from across the room, hardly out of his teens. He will be our interpreter.

"It's hard work and you get dirty," Ben tells Quang of the laborer's job he has available with his small home building company. "But it's good work." As soon as possible, we will find the family a place to live. In the meantime they will stay with us. A furrow creases Quang's brow. He looks hot inside his light shirt, uneasy.

Will he have enough money to feed his family? he wants to know. Kim is a tailor. Will there be a job for Kim?

We struggle for vocabulary. My grandfather, an immigrant from Russia, was a tailor himself. That meant not only fixing clothes but being able to make them from scratch, men's suits included. My grandmother was a seamstress, able to make dreses but not suits. Unlikely Kim is really a tailor. A seamstress then? A sewing machine operator, doing piecework? Even the interpreter struggles for words. Kim speaks no English herself.

"I don't see how there can be a job for her," Ben says. "Not until she learns the language."

But Quang is skeptical. "Will he have enough money?" the interpreter asks again.

"He should," says Ben.

Steve begins to whimper. Without being asked, Minh and Lan whisk him off, toying with the sound of his name. "Steev-uh," says Minh. "No. Stee-v," Lan corrects. Steve quiets. They take him outside, to the small strip of grass between the building and the parking lot, walking him on a narrow lawn enclosed by the hanging strips of sheets. I follow. Steve is content. I slip back inside.

These are the concerns: money, geography, the weather.

"Where is your town?" the interpreter asks.

"Crestville is in Maryland," says Ben, drawing a makeshift map.

"What is the weather like?"

"Like here. In winter, cold...for three months." Ben holds up three fingers. "Saigon is hot." Everyone nods. "There are 40,000 people in Crestville," Ben says, writing the numbers on his map. "One hundred thousand in the county. Baltimore is here, one hour away. Baltimore is a big city. Crestville is small." Everyone looks so serious, nodding, looking at the map. After a summer of waiting, how strange to be here at last, settling the terms of Quang's future across a language gap and ten thousand miles of thought. I float between the conversation at hand and my own lingering question: is that what we really want?

Much as I realize it is a poor time to ponder this, I am suddenly aware that Ben has been our prime mover all along, that I have only tagged along for the ride. Back in the spring, when the news of the 100,000-odd refugees and their flight from a falling Saigon surfaced in the papers, Ben was mildly interested in the sponsorship program. The refugees would be brought to temporary resettlement centers in the States. From there they would be matched with sponsors throughout the country, individuals and churches who would help them get started, who would see them through the first difficult months. The sponsors would have no legal obligation to support the refugees, but there would be a moral one, until they could fend for themselves. Ben had started his homebuilding business only three years before, and it was still very small, but he could always use a good laborer. Besides, he had been to Vietnam and knew something of the culture. Why not?

His brother Larry told him that his motive was guilt, an accusation Ben publicly denied. Privately, he admitted that was part of it. Working as a Marine lieutenant with Vietnamese ARVN units in 1967 and '68, he'd been impressed with the graciousness of the Vietnamese people. "Of all the people I worked with, the Koreans, the Aussies and the Americans, the South Vietnamese were the most passive," he would say, "but also the most basically *nice*. You *do* feel guilty leaving them stranded like that. You feel you've got to take the responsibility."

With motives like that, who was *I* to say no? Aside from Russian grandparents, my contact with other cultures was limited to sharing a lab bench in college with the daughter of an Indonesian diplomat. I was no political activist, either. By the time the demonstrations against the war began at the University of Maryland in the spring of 1970, I was a graduate student seven months pregnant with our

6

daughter, Lisa, teaching three sections of sophomore English. I found Kent State upsetting, but had no feelings at all about Cambodia. I taught all through the student boycott of clases only because Ben was so deeply opposed to the demonstration—and because I thought it unlikely anyone would do physical damage to a woman as obviously pregnant as I was. And now, five years later, mother of three, I told myself contact with people from another culture would be good for the children...and I, ready for a new experience, would be willing to go along.

Still more curious than committed, we called our congressman for details of the sponsorship program. We were referred to Catholic Charities in Baltimore, which sent an eager young woman to interview us one afternoon in early June. Lisa and Mike, 5 and 4, ran around the yard like maniacs while we sat at the picnic table trying to eat lunch. Steve, seven months old then and usually placid, whined. The young woman told us there had been reports of one sponsor sending a refugee family to work all day, then locking them in a trailer at night...and so the personal visit. Ben proceeded to espouse his personal philosphy of sponsorship amid the din. He would provide a job and help the family until they could get on their feet, hopefully within a few weeks of arrival. We would find housing and act as a buffer with authorities, but we would not support them. The salary from the job would do that. Ben saw himself as a sort of bridge between two cultures. He hoped he understood enough to help ease the way of a refugee into the American system. Lisa attempted a cartwheel on the lawn. Steve cried. The girl from Catholic Charities left—with the impression, we thought, that we probably weren't charitable enough...and who knows, with those undisciplined children maybe we would lock our family in a trailer at night, too. It was reassuring to find out differently, though not until early this month. The computer had found us a match.

And so on August 5 we threaded our way through the muggy Pennsylvania countryside, Mike and Lisa home (blissfully) with a babysitter, Steve asleep in my arms, concerned with practical matters. We knew almost nothing of the family—only their ages and that Quang had listed carpentry as one of his job skills. Would he want to come to Crestville, to work as a laborer on a construction crew? If so, how soon would we be able to find the family an apartment? Neither Ben nor I enjoyed long-term guests. What would it be like to entertain a houseful of foreigners?

At the guard post marking the Indiantown Gap reservation proper, a uniformed sentry gave us directions to the visitor center. We started off past fleets of Army vehicles, stared down by soldiers in fatigues, who were ostensibly trying to rejuvenate the road.

"At least this must look very familiar to the refugees," Ben told me. "The choppers, the constant presence of the military, all the equipment. It looks just like Vietnam."

I am still sometimes bewildered by Ben's Vietnam experience—his perception of it and mine. When I first met him he had just come to Headquarters Marine Corps near Washington, a first lieutenant back from his 13-month tour in Vietnam. Trucks would backfire on the highway not far from his apartment and he would jump, then catch himself so quickly I knew it happened only if I was sitting close enough to him to feel it. From his flinching I drew fearful pictures, but he denied them. Conditioned response, he would say, which he hadn't time to unlearn. The war was good for him, nutritive. Fun? And he distrusted me, I think, for what I was then—an instructor of English at the University of Maryland, teaching those liberal arts students he viewed in a hostile lump, draft dodgers all. When I defended them he cast me as an anti-war activist, though I didn't even read the newspapers. We fought the year away. How we ended up mates instead of enemies is still a mystery. I was the city girl from Washington, from a liberal background, Jewish, politically apathetic; he was the conservative Midwestern Catholic. The classic mismatch. Seven years later Ben's feelings about the war still elude me. Part of the reason I went along with this sponsorship scheme, I think, is gratitude that his way of coping with it is not guilt, not self-hate, but something neat and practical...helping somebody. So here we were.

Like the other resettlement centers, Indiantown Gap was a decaying World War II military base, outdated and shabby with disuse, a ghost town brought suddenly back to life. Beside us stretched rows of decrepit frame barracks, where the refugees lived, and administrative buildings marked with their functions in English and Vietnamese. All had once been painted white. Now the paint was chipping, peeling, leaving gray wood beneath to show through. The area around each building was cordoned off with white sheets that were threaded everywhere, forming barriers between housing and off-limits territories, between us and the refugees, even between public buildings and their parking lots. Beyond the sheets, refugees milled in droves, sitting on the steps of the barracks, hanging up laundry, watching groups of children playing on the grass. Just as I'd thought.

"It's a benevolent prison, probably," Ben said, "but it still looks like a prison." A crowded one. In one of the buildings where we stopped to ask for directions, even the corridors were jammed with refugees filling out forms. Everyone seemed slightly disoriented, as if there were too many people to deal with and too much to do to keep it all in perspective. So when we reached the visitor center it was prisoners we expected, worn and bedraggled. Even the building itself echoed decay: an old club with the inevitable chipping paint outside and inside, sparse, forbidding furnishings—picnic tables and vinyl covered chairs, sticky to the touch. The administrators had not had the presence of mind to locate Kim and Quang in advance as scheduled. We waited, pacing up and down in front of whirring fans (no air-conditioner here), watching two boys engaged in a ping-pong game, comforting a restless Steve.

"Maybe they don't want to tell them the sponsors are here until they actually arrive," Ben said. "Maybe they've had so many no-shows that they just wait until you're here." We nodded at each other. Feeling, perhaps, just a little proud of ourselves for showing up at all? And then they arrived, looking more on top of the situation than we were, in fine clothes we have yet to see again, whose origin is still a mystery, and took command of the interview as if it were no more than an ordinary social event, even Quang's nervousness melting away as we went on.

An hour passes, more. Ben speaks of shovelling dirt and staining siding, of nailing down floor boards. Of unromantic work. "I will try to give you what I would want someone to give me," he says. "A chance."

Quang cannot know how strongly Ben feels about this. Four years ago when he went into business for himself, building vacation cabins not far from here, we were down to our last thirty-four dollars before Ben was given a chance to make good. He had to pay off his land to get clear title before he could sell his first cabin. All the banks in town had written him off as a maverick. Mike and Lisa were both under two, I was unemployed, and we were one week away from having to live on air. Finally a local insurance agent lent him the money at 20 percent, though the going rate at the time was about half that. Ben was grateful. Twenty percent was better than bankruptcy, and besides, what's a little usury among friends? The insurance agent slunk around, hoping Ben would default and leave him his collateral: forty acres of waterfront property and a nice cabin. Undaunted, Ben headed for work each morning, wearing carpenter's apron and cut-offs, sure that with enough effort and the remotest chance, he could do anything., Fortunately, he pulled it off. He sold 25 cabins, paid off the loan, and got out of the vacation home business just before it took a nose-dive in the 1974 recession, with enough money to begin building the regular single-family houses he does now. This is his idea of a chance, risks and all. He is not much for handouts. I wonder if Quang has any idea.

As Ben and Quang talk, the girls entertain Steve. Kim and I study each other quietly. When our eyes meet, my inclination is to look quickly away, but Kim is not so easily frightened. She looks at me directly and smiles. I am charmed.

One final item of business. Kim has an uncle or cousin. The interpreter is not sure which: the words *uncle* and *cousin* seem to be interchangeable. What is important is that he is a relative, part of the family, and must be provided for. Though they have not seen him since Guam, they know he is in this country and want to find him so he can join them in Crestville. Will this be agreeable to Ben? Ben nods and asks for more details. In Vietnam the uncle worked with airplanes, the interpreter says. He is not very old, in his 20's. Younger than Quang? No one is sure.

The interpreter translates; Quang nods. The men stand and shake hands, as if they have reached an agreement. But how much has gotten through? How much English does the interpreter know, this slip of a refugee himself? We are never to know. We drive to the Catholic Conference office to tell them to process the papers. It will take two weeks for the family's clearance to come through, they say. They will call us. In the meantime, they will also try to locate the uncle or cousin, Fon, whose full name Kim has written down. We wave goodbye for now, anxious to talk among ourselves.

"I was impressed," Ben says in the car. "He asked the right questions. He was concerned for his family, that he would be able to support them. He was worried about Kim working. Over there there's no way they could make it without both of them working."

"You should have told them *I* don't work," I say.

"Yes, I should."

"He was pretty nervous at first," I say, not realizing that later it will be his very calmness that disturbs.

"Well, wouldn't you be nervous? After all, he is negotiating for his life."

Two weeks pass, during which I am to busy too remember my bewilderment over the family's attractiveness, their poise, the newness of their clothes. And now, tonight, the Vietnamese rock tapes bring it all back. Beneath the surface there has been too much I do not understand. The clothes we saw at Indiantown Gap seem to have disappeared; they must have been borrowed after all. Each member of the family has only a few outfits—the girls their traditional silky black pants with the tunic overblouse and a few items of American dress; Quang several pairs of trousers and some shirts. None of them have shoes, only sandals. I collect castoffs from the neighbors, thinking they will need them, but I have not seen them used. Why pack tapes when the sparse room in the hand luggage could have been filled with clothes? Why pack the tapes at all?

I try to imagine what they must have been thinking when they left, to act as they did. Kim, a bride, is staying with her family in Saigon while Quang commands a personnel carrier farther north, at Da Nang. Suddenly the army in the north is routed. After 20 years of war, the fall, which even the North Vietnamese expected to take months, has taken hours. The enemy has streamed across the DMZ and down from Cambodia. Now they are travelling south in force, throwing the country into panic. Hearing the news, Quang and the others in his unit make their plans. Together they will sail south to Saigon, to gather as much of their families as they can. Then they will put out to sea. Quang goes to the house where Kim's father lives with his two wives, his nine children, a maiden aunt or two. His own parents live and farm deep in the country, inaccessible. But Kim's father has decided his family should disperse in different directions. Most of them will stay behind with him, while he uses his embassy connections to get out. Only Kim and her two sisters will go with Quang out to sea, where they expect U.S. Navy ships to pick them up. Those who do best on the outside will help the others.

And here—as I imagine them packing quickly—I want to see Kim and Quang preparing to leave Vietnam with the same urgency my grandfather fled Russia sixty years ago. His is the only escape story I know; I want to see the parallels. Grandpa, a Jew, had his own dire choices: to leave or be inducted into the Russian army for life. He took with him his illegal passport, purchased through proper channels, money to bribe the border guards and pay for his boat ticket once he reached France, protective clothing, and some food—whatever might keep him going through perilous times. Was Kim and Quang's plight any less desperate? Though they could not know it yet, their trip was to be a long one—a day or two at sea in the crowded personnel carrier, rescue by the Navy, a long ocean journey to Subic Bay in the Philippines; from there by plane to Guam, where they stayed a month; and finally to Indiantown Gap, the resettlement center in Pennsylvania. There in Saigon they must have had barely time to think. Suddenly refugees, taking to the sea, uncertain of their fate, what would they carry with them? Certainly not a boxful of records.

So here I must be wrong. They cannot have seen their situation as I do, to bring records instead of survival items. While our American newspapers painted the military pullout in shades of gloom, Kim and Quang must have viewed it as something other than Americans leaving in abject defeat. What? Americans less humbled than simply tired of their war games, going home to enjoy their wealth? That seems to ring true. The Americans would leave, taking those Vietnamese who wished to go with them, and the rest would take care of themselves. An uncertain sea journey? Hardship and struggle in America? Not at all. To leave cooking utensils and fishing gear at home, they must have believed unquestioningly that we would pick them up at once, fly them over on our big jets, and see to the luxuries as well as necessities when they got here. Why bring rock tapes unless you expect equipment to play them on? And why bring clothes when surely they would be provided? Better to take only what could not be replaced in San Francisco—snapshots of the family, of course, and the music it would be impossible to buy in American record stores.

The more I think about it, the more this makes sense. It is the only way I seem able to explain the tapes and the untouched second hand clothes. And now there is a bewildering shopping trip to add to my confusion, which Kim and I made this morning for the underwear she and the girls have forgotten to bring.

Leaving the children with Minh and Lan, the two of us went to Taylor's, our one remaining "nice" department store in the city. All the rest have moved out to the mall. No matter, Kim loves it. From department to department she goes, ignoring the underwear which is our mission, flipping through the coat racks, fingering leather handbags, motioning me over to see what I thought. "You like?" she asks interminably, and I nod, trying to get her to pay attention to what we are doing. I discover her favorite color is red. She picks up soft red sweaters and looks fondly at the long red dresses already being shown for formal wear. "You like?" she keeps asking, and finally I begin to feel uncomfortable, not understanding the cause of all this interest, and wanting to get finished, too, because there are other errands to run. Kim is so cheerful—I put it down to that. Or maybe there are no such department stores in Saigon, maybe everything is bought in the market. I buy the underwear at last, and we go, the puzzle buried under a mound of other chores but hanging there, making me uneasy. Now I begin to understand. The neighbors' clothes sit in the closet because Kim expects me to buy new ones, much as her breeding forbids her to ask outright. We thought we were so clever, laying down our philosophy at Indiantown Gap, but if anything got through it wasn't enough to counter her own preconceptions. Not only is America rich, but Americans as well. Sponsors.

One more thought: where my grandfather had brothers already settled in Chicago, to tell him what it was really like, that no gold flowed in the streets, the refugees have no one. Grandpa knew even as he sailed from France in steerage that his brother was making meager earnings as a shoemaker's apprentice and living in a small room in a boarding house, where he spent his evenings studying English grammar. How many settled Vietnamese have been in this country over the years to tell Kim and Quang the same thing? I don't know of a single one. So here they are, aware only that America is rich. When Quang asked us at Indiantown Gap about money and we said he should have enough, maybe we should have spelled out exactly what that meant. Since he has come here, he has put aside his concern for food; now it is the tape deck he wants to buy. No wonder they have been so calm, so gracious these three days. I have seen them braving the storm with determined good cheer, only to find that for them the storm has never existed. They have come not prepared for struggle, but only to partake of our plenty. To us falls the task of re-education. It is a frightening thought.

TWO

Thursday night, the music over, everyone in bed. We have moved Steve into our room so Kim and Quang can have his. It is hard to talk without waking him, but we whisper long into the night, trying to understand. Where I react to the tapes and all they suggest with anger, with suspicion, Ben tries to understand. "You have to try to picture how it was for them in Vietnam," he says. "They probably never saw any Americans who *didn't* have a tape deck."

Here is the picture he draws, of a provincial county seat called Tam Ky, just north of the middle of the country, built along the main road from south of Saigon to Hanoi, Route 1. Ben is stationed about five miles away, on Hill 35—the hills are numbered according to the markings on their topographical maps—which his men share with a Vietnamese ARVN unit. Coincidentally, both Kim and Quang were born there. Kim's parents soon moved south to Saigon, so her father could take a government job, but Quang's family still live and farm there. The terrain is very flat, rice fields and fruit trees. To the west, four or five miles in the distance, are the mountains, visible from everywhere in the town. To the east another five miles, is the sea. Route 1 runs through the center of town, a paved strip twelve feet wide. The side streets are mud. The villagers have no cars, but many of them ride bikes or mopeds, and there are some three-wheeled commercial vehicles on the roads. Along Route 1 sit blocks of adobe shops, with tin roofs and wood floors. They are the best buildings in town.

In the morning, market. A central open-air place, with hawkers selling food. Women come from a three-mile radius to shop. They walk home with their purchases in baskets, the baskets balanced on yokes slung across their shoulders.

Everyone farms. Water buffalo dot the landscape, a measure of a family's affluence. The rice paddies are roughly 300' x 300', with little dikes around them for irrigation. There are no pumps. Two men

15

stand on the bank, dipping and spilling water from one paddy to another. They use five-gallon baskets attached to ropes and pulleys, to guide the water across the paddies for 15 or 20 feet. It can take five or six hours to change the water level.

Some of the troopers think the method of irrigation is ingenious. Ben does not. "The villagers would ride their bikes or their mopeds out to the paddies and then pump by hand," he says. "They never thought about using their motors to do the work."

In the morning and in the late afternoon until dark, people work in the rice paddies. During the heat of the day they disappear into their houses—one-room mud huts about 15' x 20' or so, with thatched roofs. No indoor plumbing, no glass in the windows, no doors. They cook over wood fires, or on primitive stoves. Some of the huts have furniture: a chair or two. The very nicest have wooden floors; the majority have dirt. Life is slow and easy. Nobody has much of anything. There is no medical care, no dentists. Those whose teeth have rotted chew betel nut for the narcotic effect. Almost all the old people chew it.

And then into this lethargic atmosphere come the Americans, landing at Da Nang. We arrive with jeeps, tanks, trucks, watches, radios. Even in the most desolate outposts, we always have beer. The actual fighting is done in the jungle, or out in the hills. Life in the village is relaxed. Our troopers give away cigarettes and extra C-rations. They play with their toys: cameras brought from R and R in Japan, jewelry from Bangkok, tape decks from Hong Kong. Our medical corpsmen give out medicines. The villagers take our discarded wood scraps to fix up their homes. They recycle our beer cans by building walls out of them. The Americans are rich, rich enough to throw away their wealth.

In return for money and trinkets, the Vietnamese provide small services. "Even the lowliest trooper didn't do his own laundry," says Ben. "The Vietnamese *mama-sans* would come around and do it for maybe fifty cents." The troopers' problem is too much money, too few places to spend it.

On Hill 35, Ben's platoon has half the occupied area. The other half is run by a Vietnamese ARVN unit. "When the Vietnamese troops did something wrong, the officers would beat the hell out of them. They were a lot more vicious to their guys than we were," Ben says.

One night a Vietnamese soldier is found in an American bunker, stealing radios and food. "Our troopers wouldn't just take and beat the guy up for the hell of it," Ben tells me. Instead they return him to his own commanding officer, who beats him for the offense. The Americans feel vaguely guilty. "Later our guys made him sort of a mascot. They'd give him cigarettes and try to get him drunk on beer—which wasn't very hard. In a condescending way, of course, they kind of liked him."

This is how we were: not perfect, not heartless. It wasn't that simple, Ben insists. You can't characterize everything in terms of My Lai.

"The people saw us as generous and friendly, sort of Teddy-bearish, with all kinds of riches and able to solve any problem. If we had to blow up a vehicle in the field to keep it out of enemy hands, we would just get another. That's how rich we were," says Ben. No wonder Kim looks at red dresses, thinking I will buy them. No wonder they have brought their tapes. They think it goes with the territory.

Now, with this picture in mind, I see what Kim and Quang have been doing—reacting with delight to our riches. And also—here's the rub—with distress to what they perceive as lack of it. There have been so many little incidents; only now it begins to fall into place.

There was, for instance, their arrival Tuesday afternoon. We'd had an uneventful two-hour drive back from Indiantown Gap, children and all. Only Lisa, upset by the strangeness of the situation, had an outburst of crying and thumb-sucking. Everyone else was quiet, except Quang, who exchanged small talk with Ben, the two of them struggling with their ten-word vocabulary. Kim and Minh slept; Lan, thoughtful, stared out the window.

And then, arriving here, the family became suddenly animated, all smiles, relieved. Before them stood our house, finished only last fall, dark contemporary lines rising against a half-acre of trees. Our block curves away to the east, street dappled in sunlight, a few big houses filling in the woods. Ben says our house is like a Saigon mansion. We show them their rooms—Steve's room for Kim and Quang, Mike's for the girls—large and filled with light. They settle in at once. Kim even reorganizes the closet (much to my chagrin—I should have done it myself), but with such delight that I can only be as happy about it as she is. I begin to understand what Ben means about Vietnamese graciousness.

Later I show them the workings of everything—showers, washing machine, heat light in the bathroom—not knowing whether I am making a fool of myself or not, but afraid not to demonstrate after hearing that the Vietnamese are often unfamiliar with all our American gadgetry. They smile, enjoying. Only the vacuum cleaner and the dishwasher are really strange, but they delight in it all, part of the riches. Minh and Lan laugh to discover the dishes need only to be rinsed before being stacked in the dishwasher, not cleansed thoroughly with detergent as well. It is a game of luxury. We could have brought them to a crowded garret after all, and instead we have turned out to be just what they must have hoped. Kim relaxes and surveys our vegetable garden in back with approval, pointing out the tomatoes and cucumbers, telling me, more in gestures than in words, that these things also grew in back of her father's house in Saigon.

In the giddiness that follows, Quang makes bold to tell us that Kim does not like fish, which I have served for dinner along with vegetables and rice, trying to strike a familiar culinary chord. We are relieved: the children who also dislike fish, have agreed to put up with it if necessary out of courtesy. We are flattered that they felt comfortable enough to make coments, and yet I am troubled, too. Would *I* admit dissatisfacton with my first meal as a guest in a foreign house? I dish out ice cream for dessert; Quang approves. "We have this often," he says, "in my country." The undercurrent stays. I feel briefly as if he is trying to manipulate me. Serve this, here is something we like. That we can do without. As if it is my duty to provide not just nourishment but pleasure. And I am briefly annoyed.

Our first night sets the precedent for household chores. Dinner is over and the girls jump into action. The dishes are cleared, the table wiped, the work done with record speed. Kim manages the girls with the efficiency of a seasoned administrator. We are all talk and laughter, separate languages aside. Only Lan has a moment of sadness: she excuses herself and takes a short walk in the yard.

"She misses too much her friend," says Quang, telling us of a girl Lan has spent the last two months with at Indiantown Gap. Then Lan returns, once more composed, ready to help. Our operation moves with the efficiencey of a well-oiled machine. I have learned that Kim is the second oldest of nine children. Her older sister has been married for some years, so at home Kim is in charge, second only to her mother. I see them waving at her in the snapshots she has brought from home, smiling from the balcony of their two-story house in the city. Along with her delight in our things, there is also Kim's breeding, evident even on that first night, the easy cheerfulness that moves her sisters with a word and a smile, with such lack of effort. I am impressed.

And the next day, Wednesday, I learn a little more of this city girl, of what she expects. Quang has gone to work ("There's no point in him staying home," Ben says), Minh and Lan agree to babysit, and Kim and I go to the grocery store, which Kim is anxious to see. Apparently they have talked about our odd marketing practices at Indiantown Gap. In America the goods sit on the shelves, and there is no haggling over prices. She brings along a paperback English grammar book, with a picture of a woman standing under a Check Out sign, and some common grocery terms below. "Now," she says earnestly as we get into the car, "we go to check out." I shake my head. Kim is dismayed. She listens, puzzled. The check out is only *part* of the store, where the bill is paid. The store itself is a supermarket, a grocery store. A moment of blankness. "Ah," she smiles at last. "Supermarket." Already her smile is entrenched in our language: everything will be all right. If this is culture shock, she hides it well. Probe as I will, the cheerfulness seems genuine. It would be impossible not to like Kim.

We make the shopping trip a major one, everything from milk to fruit. I want Kim to get a good idea of the system. She examines rows of packaged spices and looks askance at a cellophane-wrapped roast I choose. She soon develops the courage to help, frowning at my lettuce, replacing it, returning with a firmer, better head. The store is to her liking: it yields up more of its bounty at each turn. Then, acclimated, she hunts up and down the aisles in search of something. At last she finds it, a pair of rubber gloves to wear while doing dishes, to protect her long nails and enormous opal ring.

We finish. Clearly she feels she has mastered the American marketing system. "*Now* we go to the checkout," I say. And finding this very funny, she helps me pile the groceries onto the counter, including the protective gloves that would surely seem superfluous to a girl expecting to live in poverty, to hand wash her laundry and scrub her floors.

There was more: for lunch that day, we went out to the building site, to show the girls where Ben and Quang work. We took the children and a picnic lunch with us, only to find Ben away on an errand when we arrived. The building site is a long treed street with several houses finished and occupied. Farther down the road is an excavated lot, stark clay with a half-finished house on it, baking in the sun. Next door, a second house, under roof but not yet drywalled.

The girls step outside with the children for a moment, then Minh and Lan retreat to the shade of the car, apparently finding the heat no pleasure after the tropics. Kim, ever gracious, endures. When Ben returns, we eat on the bare plywood floor of the house that has just been put under roof, using the exposed studs as backrests. Kim's silky black pants become white with sawdust. The episode does not phase her good nature, but it is clearly not what she expected. Is she surprised, then, to find Ben in work clothes instead of a tie, lunching in the field rather than an office? I think so. Everyone seems glad to return to the house.

Friday was worse. On Friday, unsuspecting, I dealt Kim a major blow which made me realize there was more to her expectation than nice clothes and smooth hands and maybe a cassette player. On Friday afternoon, for the first time, I took her to see an apartment.

The incident catches me off balance. I forget Kim knows nothing of housing. I have been looking at apartments for weeks, since the day after our meeting at Indiantown Gap, answering every ad, trying to find something suitable. Much as we like the family, we also value our privacy. Steve has been waking during the night off and on since he's been in our room...and though having the family is so much easier than we could have imagined, how can they understand what life here is like until they are on their own?

So I have been looking for housing, and so far it's been a night-mare. I started out naive, never having to look before at apartments in the price range Quang can afford on his laborer's salary, and am only gradually getting educated: what slums people advertise in the local classifieds. And even then the landlords hand-pick their tenants. "Are they black?" they ask me boldly over the phone, suspicious because I am calling for someone not yet in town. Discrimination laws seem not to have trickled down—or out—as far as Crestville. Rather than mention them (cheap housing is scarce; what good would it do?), I try my charm. I go on about the plight of the poor refugees, trying to wangle an appointment. It doesn't always work. On an ascending scale of 1 to 10, black is one. Vietnamese is...what? Two? Two and a half?

All the same, I've seen enough places to get the general idea. One, an upstairs flat billed as two-bedroom, has a second bedroom that really turns out to be a dining area, open to the hall. "Well, you could *use* it as a bedroom," the landlady says. I mention that the kitchen, a sliver of a room, hardly qualifies as a dining area. She shrugs, leading me into the bathroom—rusted pipes, falling plaster—and out onto the back porch. The porch overflows with trash, a good month's worth, scooped up hastily after the last tenant's departure, stuffed into plastic garbage bags. I leave huffily and cannot understand her bewilderment until I've looked at a few more places, much worse.

The one that sticks in my mind most vividly is a row house, on a block set between slums and suburbs. Three spacious bedrooms up, living, dining and kitchen down. A nice front porch and a back yard. Here's the catch: it is also a burnt-out shell. Inside, last winter, the ductwork caught on fire, burning holes in the living room wall and the wall of the master bedroom. The good doctor who owns it isn't planning to fix it. He's offering it cheaply, he says, and if the tenants want to do something with it, fine. If not, then obviously there will be no heat. He doesn't mention this though.

By the time Kim and Quang actually arrived, we'd given up on the local classifieds and run an ad ourselves. Friday we got our first call, and so for the first time Kim came with me to look. Actually the place wasn't bad. A second-floor apartment over a store on the west end, two nice bedrooms, big kitchen, sun roof outside for hanging wash. But Kim, who is always pleasant, always smiling, goes suddenly blank, her face a round white moon, taking in the rooms without expression.

When we get home the questions start. She points to the yard. "How much for this?" she asks. How much for a dishwasher? How much for a house? And suddenly it occurs to me: so far we are her only model of American life. She has expected a place like ours. No one has told her that immigrants, much less refugees, do not step effortlessly into the comfortable middle class. Her surprise is so genuine, her disappointment so real that I cannot help feeling sorry for her, at the same time that I am vaguely annoyed. I want her to understand that the good life has to be earned. At her age Ben and I had nothing either. It came slowly, by degrees: cramped apartments, long work hours, years with run-down secondhand cars. Then I remind myself that what seems like gold-digging is guileless. It is only that Kim thought she would have everything...and it is not to be. Ben and I confer quickly while he shaves after work. After dinner he sits the family down to prepare a budget.

They have, aside from Quang's salary every week, $1,200 in government subsidy coming soon: $300 for each person. That means when we do find an apartment, they will be able to pay any security deposit and cover any unexpected expenses that may come up. Otherwise, the subsidy money will go into their savings. Eventually they will want a car (neither of them drive yet) and other things. Ben wants them to live on the weekly check.

Pencil and paper in hand, Ben shows Quang how to allot so much money for rent, so much for food, so much for bus'fare and miscellaneous. "Every week, put a little into savings," Ben says. "Even if it's only two dollars, it's very important to save."

Quang understands at once: he is good with figures. And Kim sits next to him, still pale, the notion hanging heavy, perhaps, that life will not be easy. Or perhaps it is too soon for American dollars to mean much to her. They are only numbers on a page. Until she has to pay for her own food, how can she really know what the numbers will buy?

"They've got to learn to become capitalists in the sense of working for what they get and saving and being independent," Ben tells me tonight. "It's the only way to survive in this country." Kim is likely to be disappointed in her first apartment, but so what? They must learn that you get things by paying for them, and you pay by working hard. So simple. Always before I've been irritated by what I think is Ben's out-and-out subscription to the work ethic, but tonight I find myself agreeing with him. Let them slug it out for themselves; it will be good for them. Then I back off, still that city-bred liberal at heart, suspicious of tried-and-true Americanisms. The work ethic is working well enough for us now that Ben has parlayed those vacation cabins into a legitimate homebuilding business... but God knows it doesn't work for everybody. My father had a whole string of jobs through the years to support his career as a professional musician. Wednesday and Saturday matinees at the legitimate theaters where he played and daytime rehearsals for the monthly classical concerts at the art gallery never quite jibed with his nine-to-five jobs. It's been satisfying for him, I think, but hard on my mother, who's always had to work for money rather than love.

Maybe I'm oversensitive. Ben likes to shrug my writing off as a hobby because the money I get from the Washington papers for my real estate articles is sporadic and the magazine assignments so hit-or-miss he refuses to count them. His attitude annoys me. If it doesn't yield enough cold cash to support us, it's frivolous, he believes. I'm not sure I want Kim and Quang to think this way. On the other hand, I don't want them to expect too much, and particularly not to expect it from *me*, for purely selfish reasons. (So I can have enough time to engage in that frivolous hobby of mine, writing?)

In the back of my mind there's something more serious...that someone with an accent, from a different culture, no matter what his hopes, might be able to go only so far. Grandpa, for all the sweat he put into his tailor shop over the years, reaped only modest comforts. Can Quang expect more? (Is my thinking a kind of bigotry?) Already it looks like there are going to be more problems than we'd anticipated.

Ben had hoped Quang would turn out to be a good carpenter and that he'd be able to move him up quickly, out of the laborer's job he has now. Instead he's discovered Quang probably never lifted a hammer before. "Anyone with carpentry skills holds a hammer close to the end," Ben says. "An amateur has a tendency to hold it near the head. That's what Quang does." We suspect Quang thought carpentry skills might prove useful. He had to put *something* on his work experience sheet. How do you translate duties as a Vietnamese navy lieutenant into a paying civilian job which doesn't require much English? So now Ben is paying him about fifty percent more than he normally would give someone with no experience, and waiting for him to learn.

"I don't really mind that," he says. "I recognize this is part charity. But I'd like to see him earn his money in six months." It's to be no easy climb through the ranks. I wonder if Quang will be willing to stick it out.

And then through all this (our little unpleasant surprises) there are also the pleasures, which more than compensate. Minh and Lan have brought with them their astonishing way with children, which we have read about but, until now, never seen. Without being urged or asked, they have taken them over completely and charmed them so that I rarely know they're here. Steve is rocked to sleep at least ten times a day in the living room or, failing that, lured into complacency on the glider section of the swing in the yard. With Mike, they tease. "You girl?" they ask, so that he, thinking they don't understand the word in English, very patiently corrects. "No, I'm a boy," he says. "A *boy*." And they do it over and over again until Mike pretends he is angry and stomps away, secretly glad for the attention. Even Lisa has quickly come around. Minh and Lan regard the children as a delight, never a chore. It's like having live-in help.

And Kim, aside from her love of nice things, is an endless source of amazement to me, handling the girls with a diplomacy that escapes most people twice her age. Except for the incident at the apartment, she has seemed to float through all the changes with a smile.

In the mornings we've begun a program of English lessons, using texts I've bought from the director of the foreign language school at the Lutheran church. When tutors are found, they will be able to go to the church twice a week for more formal instruction. In the meantime we go through our routine: "This is the bird, this is the tree...." Sometimes Minh, especially, is too shy to repeat, but Kim (whose pronunciation is even better than Quang's, and who understands much more than she can say), will try anything, until the lessons become a great game and the girls are learning in spite of themselves.

Or when Minh and Lan seem sad, as they sometimes do, Kim lets them tease her. The girls rinse the dishes, and I ask Kim what she would like to do in this country. She wants to be an American singer, say Minh and Lan.

"Oh, do you sing?" I ask.

"*Titi*," Kim says. "A little."

"*Beaucoup!*" shout the girls. And suddenly they are cheerful as ever. Even when there is work to do, Kim gets them going with a smile. A gesture, a phrase, and they are up, clearing the table, picking up the room. She seems to guide them with her charm.

Only sometimes do I see the strain she must be under. In the evenings the family has been going upstairs early, all of them talking for a while in Kim and Quang's room, then getting ready for bed. I wonder whether they do it because they are tired, or whether they feel they must keep out of the way.

Today we had a cookout at our friends' Bill and Anne's house, taking the family along. We were so stuffed afterwards that Ben and I decided to skip dinner. We put the children to bed and went to read upstairs, leaving Kim to cook for her family. She has cooked once or twice before, a chicken dish we ate yesterday, and a soup she makes for lunch, but this was the first time she had the kitchen to herself. I heard the clatter of dishes, smelled the garlic (Kim can use eight or ten cloves of garlic in a single dish and somehow make it taste good), and felt that the family was able to be itself for the first time since their arrival, laughing and helping and cleaning up. How different it must be for them here, under our shadow, than it was at home. I remind myself to arrange more occasions like this, when they can be downstairs by themselves, alone.

THREE

An odd week, lots of ups and downs. On Monday—the good news—we found an apartment which even Kim cannot help liking, it is so huge. We can thank our ad for finding it. Monday morning the owner of the building called, so we went to see it as soon as Quang came home from work. It's on the first floor of one of those big old buildings just north of downtown, a huge high-ceilinged place that must have once been an office since the rooms are laid out in a row, one in back of the other. There is a front room, three big bedrooms (one for the uncle if he ever gets here), a dining room which can become a family room since the kitchen is so big, and the eat-in kitchen. There's also a porch out back, but no yard to speak of. And the neighborhood is really quite respectable. To the north, lots of rental housing, rather expensive; two blocks to the south, the public square. There is an A & P within walking distance, as well as all the major shopping. The post office three blocks away, the main branch of the bank three and a half, and of course all the downtown stores and drugstores. Better yet, the Lutheran church, where the English classes are held, is directly across the street.

Ordinarily Quang wouldn't be able to afford this place. It rents for $175 a month. But Stevens, the landlord, was willing to let it go for $40 less if whoever rented it would do some work in return—stoke the coal furnace that heats the building in winter, and set out the garbage twice a week. (The garbage is bagged by the tenants, then thrown down a chute so that it lands on the other side of the basement from the furnace.) The place wasn't spotlessly clean, but it wasn't filthy, either, and all the walls were papered, and the rooms so big, it was irresistible. Kim was anxious to have it from the start. Now I'm glad she's been able to see a little of what else is available. If we'd been here first, she might not have been so enthusiastic.

The one sour note is that the landlord is not exactly dripping with sympathy. He's a burly gray-haired redneck, who makes it clear the only reason he's letting Quang have the apartment is because he wants someone to do the work. He and his wife own a little grocery store up on Center Street, about a mile away, and apparently he doesn't have time to stoke the furnace and tend store too. While we were there Monday evening, he took us to the basement to show Quang what had to be done—shovel the coal in, and take the cinders out. Very little of the lesson got across. And Stevens, who knew full well Quang had only been here a week and spoke very little English, soon became gruff and impatient all the same...although to his credit, he didn't try to back out of the arrangement. I told him that by the time the cold weather came Quang's English should be better and that Ben would come with him to look at the furnace when it was time to turn it on for real. We signed the lease the next day, which gives Quang the apartment as of September 1, though we know it might take some time to furnish it and get them ready to move in.

As for Quang, his introduction to American life gets less and less gentle. Stevens isn't the only one who is openly prejudiced. When Quang got here, one of Ben's brick masons told him, "I'm not going to work with no damn gook." To which Ben replied, simply, "I don't think you have a whole hell of a lot of choice." That shut the mason up.

Now the main problem is Ronny, not one of your more patient souls. Ronny has been with Ben ever since he built this house; in fact, he was the *only* one with Ben then. He's so crude that when he was working here I had to keep the kids out of earshot...but he's also steady and loyal. Ben had no choice but to put Quang on the same crew with him. Unfortunately, Ronny regards this as something of an insult. He yells at Quang for not understanding rather than explaining to him, and he regards Quang's physical smallness as a joke—God knows why. Ronny is strong, but he's only about 5'10". Ben endures, insisting that Ronny is clever with his hands and that Quang can learn a lot from him if he wants to.

"Besides, with two crews and one laborer, what else can I do?" he says...which indicates to me that Ben feels guilty about the situation, but helpless. In the meantime, Quang is apparently picking up the work quickly enough. Ronny cannot be intimidating him entirely. When I ask Ben if he is encouraged by Quang's progress, he only shrugs. "When you have someone who knows absolutely nothing to start, who's intelligent and willing to learn, naturally they improve rapidly at first," he says. "We'll have to wait and see."

At home the week has been chaotic, largely because a reporter came out to interview the family and wrote an article which ran in the local paper Tuesday night. By then we'd found the apartment, so we told her that the family was essentially without household goods. The reporter also asked us if they needed clothes...a source of confusion to me still. Between what I gathered from the neighbors before the family arrived, and what was in the boxes, there seemed to be enough to last until cold weather, though not so much for Quang, and no shoes other than sandals. I must have let my uncertainty show...a big mistake. The article brought in a great deal of clothes. By Wednesday morning we were being deluged with calls (the first one came at 6:30 a.m.), with people wanting to bring things over or—more commonly—have us pick them up. Mostly clothes, of course, everything from size 16 housedresses (the article had specified the girls were small) to beat-up bedroom slippers, mutilated pink fluff. Along with umbrellas, pots and pans, knick-knacks, irons, you name it, some of it not so bad. The many moods of American charity.

Some of the callers are beyond belief. The 6:30 a.m. caller was a lady who phoned with size 14 clothes she thought we could make over. When that didn't bring us rushing to her door, she called again, offering other things, if only we would pick them up. I finally went, and here was her donation: mildewed rugs from the depths of her basement, a plastic table cloth with holes in it, a box of buckwheat pancake mix, bought by mistake and too valuable to pitch out. All of it garbage.

It's odd who donates the best things. A woman in a tenement row house gave us some good dishes and a clock that works, all of it clean and neatly wrapped. Only the rich seem unashamed to let their castoffs go unwashed. As for the drop-offs, Minh and Lan answer the door smiling, and take everything in with gracious thank-yous, no matter how awful it is. Then they cart it up to the bedrooms, where it disappears as if into a great hole. Even the best clothes I haven't seen them use. Maybe they are waiting to move into the apartment, where they can sort through it all without the fear of insulting us in case they decide to throw some of it away. I try to explain we will not be upset, but I'm sure they don't know quite what to think.

In the midst of this confusion, Ben came down with a whopper of a stomach virus which shot his temperature up to 103° and left him lying helplessly in bed while Kim and I ran errands and Minh and Lan babysat. This is Ben's first illness in three years. To add to the bedlam, other refugees we didn't even know were in town have discovered the family through the article and have been calling ever since, along with the donators. I never know when I answer whether I'll be greeted in English or Vietnamese. It's not that there are so many other refugees—maybe five families in all—as that they regard the phone as a great toy. Now that they have discovered Kim and the girls, and since the women have very little to do, they call back and forth incessantly, several times a day. The upshot of this is that I have been out of the house most of the time, gathering donations, while Kim and the girls have been spending a great deal of time on the phone. Ben has been lying in bed waiting to be served aspirin and soup, and the house has gone from reasonably clean to pig-sty filthy.

It isn't that the girls don't try to help. They do: they jump into action the moment they see me begin to pick up or whenever Kim barks an order in Vietnamese. But when we're not here, they do nothing. Perhaps so as not to offend me? They play with the children, Minh polishes her nails, and the dust gathers...along with fingerprints on the windows and toys strewn across the whole downstairs. Ben says I have to ask for help ("You can't expect them to be clairvoyant"), and I'm sure he's right. But how to go about it tactfully and still be understood? In the meantime the vacuum cleaner is a great source of fascination—oh! look at that—but not to the point that the girls actually use it. We cope, but not as smoothly as we did before the community descended on us.

And now, because of all the publicity, we have discovered the churches. I don't know if this is going to be good or bad. On Friday morning when I'd had all I could handle of picking up donations, a woman named Vikki Anderson phoned, who said she was part of a group who called themselves the Indochinese Task Force. Apparently a group of volunteers from different churches have formed a committee to help the refugees. They're setting up a clothing bank in one of the church social halls so the refugees can take what they need, and they're helping to run errands. Welcome relief. Vikki sent a woman to get some things a lady from the other end of town wanted us to pick up. (These donors always seem to have deadlines, especially the ones with worthless trash: you can have such and such if you get here by ten o'clock). So that was nice.

What is not so nice is that we are running already into church philosophy about how to handle the refugees, which is a little different from ours. All the other refugee families in town are being sponsored by churches. What these churches do is take them in, either putting them in a paid-up apartment or an unused parsonage or somebody's house, and give them *everything*, at least from what we've heard so far. How long this is supposed to go on I don't know.

Yesterday I talked to a woman named Mrs. Bering, who has one of the refugee families living on the third floor of her house. Her family has been here a month, she says, and since the church doesn't believe in taking the government subsidy money, the congregation is supporting them completely. The man is working. There is also a wife, two children, and the man's younger brother, who is in high school. When I told Mrs. Bering we'd found Kim and Quang an apartment, she was obviously shocked. "We aren't planning to have our family move for a while," she said. "At least not until he can save enough money for a car, so he can drive to work."

While on the one hand this all sounds very cozy, on the other it sounds a little like blackmail. What does the church want? Converts? If so, they've certainly got their refugee family by the tail. Without the government subsidy money, they're completely under the church's thumb...for a while, at least. Show up on Sunday or else. And I wonder how realistic it is to have a whole bunch of people providing food and transportation and every other little need while you put your earnings in the bank. I wonder because now, with the piles of stuff coming into the house from our charitable local residents—and with Kim learning from her new refugee phone friends just how totally most of them are being supported—we've had our first actual confrontation about what I ought to provide for her.

It happened in the grocery store yesterday morning, in the school supply section, where Kim held up a double 8" x 10" picture frame for me to admire, with a fancy white filigree molding around it. She didn't actually ask for it until I was at the checkout counter. Then she held her finger up as if we'd forgotten something, disappeared, and returned with the frame in hand just as the last gallon of milk was rung up, pointing to it urgently. "I need," she said. Such exquisite timing! I shook my head no. "You buy this when you have your own money," I said, knowing half the words would be lost in translation. "Quang should give you some spending money to take with you when you go out." Kim's face went blank; she dropped her hand with the frame in it and took it back to the shelf. I felt as if I had slapped her.

29

Now here is the problem: I know Kim's greatest treasures at this point are her photographs, especially two large ones, one of her parents and one of her with Quang on their honeymoon. I know these are what she plans to put in the fancy frame. And the frame costs less than $5; I could easily afford it. The question is do I buy it, or do I refuse on principle, so that she will understand that, whatever other sponsors do, whatever the flood of things pouring into the house seems to indicate, all the same we expect her to support herself? Because Ben, in particular, is very serious about this business of self-sufficiency. He thinks if we foot the bill for trinkets while Quang puts his salary in the bank, we will be starting something it will be hard to end. He wants the family to learn that you don't get doodads until you can afford them. Certainly you don't beg for them. And so I say no, on principle. But it doesn't make me feel very good. In spite of her command of the girls and her incredible poise, there is something childish about Kim: she wants things with the same wide-eyed yearning Lisa does at five. It would be pleasant enough to buy them for her. And to her credit, when I say no the child in her disappears. There is no pouting, no holding a grudge. By the time we carry the groceries to the car, we are back to normal. And later Kim insists on cooking spareribs for us, trying to please. Her buoyancy almost makes me feel worse.

Dinner time: Kim prepares food with great relish, though the girls tease her that she is a terrible cook. In fact I think they are delighted to have something at least vaguely familiar once in a while. We don't have all the ingredients Kim would normally use, so she improvises with abandon. The end product tastes good enough to us, though it's full of the usual garlic, toned down with a spoonful of sugar so that our stomachs rebel only afterwards. Last night the spareribs did me in, and the heavy smell of garlic in the house seemed to compound the pain. Ben—now recovered—says when he was sick and Kim was downstairs cooking garlicky chicken soups for lunch, the smell bothered him too. Now I know how he felt. Upstairs it lingers, but it is not so strong. I went to bed early.

And while I slept, three Vietnamese women from the area came to visit, bringing more strange food with them. This time it was an old whiskey bottle full of *nuoc mam*—anchovy fish sauce—which the Vietnamese apparently pour over everything like ketchup, though how they can stand it I don't know. Kim let me smell it, a clear sour liquid with garlic and red peppers floating on top. Yuk.

Even today, the odor of garlic is still strong in the house from last night's meal. Ben says in Vietnam they could often spot the presence of the enemy by the odor of garlic and *nuoc mam*. "You could smell it 100 yards away," he says. I believe him. The house smells as if it's been invaded; I am getting weary. I know this is unsportsmanlike—imagine what it must be like for *them*—but there it is.

And one final thing. In the midst of all the activity, just when Ben was getting better, Kim developed a mysterious stomach ailment of her own. Until then, I was priding myself on how well we communicated in spite of our lack of a common language. Every day Kim tells me stories, words and gestures, until I begin to have a picture of her at home: living in her father's house in the city, helping her mother to shop and cook. Shopping is the great chore, done each morning no matter what. "Cow die today," Kim says. "Eat today." And then at home, chopping vegetables, dicing small pieces of meat. Meat is scarce, cooking takes hours. We have turkey for dinner, and Kim is astounded that we don't serve the carcass. She uses it to make a huge pot of soup. And then, reminiscing, she tells of her married sister, who lives not far away. Kim walks there often in the afternoon, though her head throbs from the heat of the sun, to play with her sister's daughter, her baby niece. Another time she tells of her father, the patriarch, very stern, motioning with her hand to show how he spanks the children, yet laughing, respectful. It is from him she has gotten her instructions, to take care of the girls.

And so I think I am beginning to understand her, until this. She takes to her bed, points to her belly to show me where it hurts. Beyond that we have no words. I feel as I do when Steve gets sick—helpless, panicky—when he is unable to do more than whine. Has she caught Ben's stomach virus? Is it serious? Do we need a doctor? Kim is so uncomplaining, I don't know what to think. She lies there in silence, impossibly pale. Then among the women who have been her phone friends since the newspaper article, we discover Yen, not a refugee but the wife of an American army sergeant, who speaks fluent English. A bi-lingual Vietnamese in Crestville! Salvation. Yen tells me it is not the flu at all, only cramps. We cure Kim easily with Midol, with a lazy day of sleep.

But the memory lingers. It is frightening not to have the words. Easy enough to talk about budgeting, about living modestly at first, about apartments and jobs...but when illness threatens we see how little gets through. A belly ache can mean anything. With all our little problems, the real issue comes down to this: having them here is weighty, like being responsible for someone else's child.

FOUR

The family is in their own apartment and the girls in school. Relief? Not exactly. Compared to this, their stay in our house was like a honeymoon, all sweetness. Now Kim expects me to drive her everywhere as before, except that to do it I have to dress all three children, go over there, pick her up, take her back. When I am not around, she talks on the phone to the other refugees, commiserating. And while she sits out her great slump in the apartment, Quang plods along at work, not exactly the hero he was three weeks ago. I know this sounds uncharitable. I *feel* uncharitable, and I'm tired. It started just before the move, when Kim was still in her post-arrival high, with household goods pouring in after the newspaper article...and me, thinking myself so clever, calling up the Rescue Mission to see if we could get the major pieces of furniture cheaply from their thrift store.

The Rescue Mission, true to its function, was very nice...too nice. Quang took $50 of the subsidy money with him to pay for whatever he bought. We figured he could afford just that much. Ben made a little speech to the effect that he should try to pay *something*, because by doing so he could keep his self-respect. Then we got to the thrift store and the mission people announced that they would refuse to accept a cent. What's a charity to do if not be charitable? Kim and Quang are obviously delighted rather than ashamed. In spite of what we have been telling them, everything is to be a giveaway. And I, embarrassed by their obvious relief, keep saying they should take only what they need, nothing extra. No matter, Kim ignores me and goes about her business, as wrapped up in the secondhand furniture as she was in the clothes at Taylor's Department Store, except that this time she will be able to choose to her heart's content. She prowls the floor, ignoring the threadbare chairs and used mattresses, managing to come up with the best pieces: a couple of solid wood dressers, an ornate porcelain lamp, a dressing table with a mirror—hardly a necessity.

"You don't really need that," I tell her pointedly.

She reexamines it. A very nice piece, considering. "I want," she says. So much for my censorship, so much for our talk of self-sufficiency. She wants. I simmer, embarrassed at what looks to me like greed. Then she finds her sofa, and I see the senselessness of my anger. The sofa is red and black, a Spanish style affair, cover worn thin, springs popping up from the frame. Once she discovers it she will have no other, though I point out better pieces here and there. She shakes her head, adamant. The sofa is red, therefore wonderful, like a worn but beloved teddy bear. Who am I to argue? West confronts East, West insisting on practicality and self-sufficiency and payment, East wanting something that will reflect even dimly her love of elaborate reds—this is to be her first home, after all—and the two of us face off over junk furniture nobody else wants anyway, with good reason. Ridiculous. We finish the errand in better humor. Now the sofa sits in Kim's living room, popping its springs, her prize.

But as for the lesson that charity must be accepted sparingly and with a bowed head, I don't know. Ben and I talk, but what the family actually sees is that the flow of goods will apparently be endless. Only when we begin bringing things from our house to the apartment so Kim can set up her kitchen do I get a good idea of the volume of it. Dishes, pots and pans, enough vases to stock a flower shop, serving pieces, two irons, you name it. There is enough to furnish two houses and still throw out the worst of it. Right before the move, Ben and Quang take the company truck to pick up some of the bigger items people have offered. There is another sofa, a dining room set, even a black-and-white TV that works perfectly once Ben hooks it up to cable. We are especially pleased about the TV since it will be a source of English coming into the house. Not Kim, though. "I like color," she says frowning, pointing to our own TV. "Like you."

So there we stand, Ben preaching hard times and self-support, Kim looking at the flood of household goods people have given her, thinking she has only scratched the surface of the mother lode. If people could give away all this, there must be more to be had if it were wanted...and better.

"*She* doesn't know how much a color TV costs," says Ben, charitable. "She thinks if someone can throw away a black-and-white set, why not color?" True, perhaps, but I think he's missed the point. Whatever happened to gratitude? Or to take it one step further, why can't we get the message across that in a crisis it's all right to tap people's sympathy once, but then you can't continue playing the same tune. You have to be content with what you get and proud enough not to ask for more.

I wish I had a picture of the first apartment Ben and I lived in just outside of Washington. Our sofa was new, a wedding present, but everything else was cast-offs, and there wasn't much of it either. No color TV, certainly. That came four years and two children later, after the vacation cabin project made good. Why does Kim think her first American apartment should come equipped with every luxury? Whatever happened to first things first?

Even now that she's spending her own money for some things, she seems to have no sense of perspective, of economy. The essentials blur into the decorative; she can't tell them apart. The apartment is almost completely equipped by the time she unpacks all the donations, but we go shopping for a few final needs, among them a potato peeler. At the store I show her one, but she shakes her head. "No. I want like you," she tells me, tapping the handle, reminding me that at home one of my potato peelers has a green plastic handle instead of a stainless one, with little flowers etched into the plastic. Not until we search the store thoroughly without success will she accept the plain handle. I tell her that plain equipment is less expensive. She shrugs and smiles, unsatisfied. Does she believe that in America we have so much that we fail to make the distinction between function and ornament? I think so. All those American cast-offs and if she's going to spend her own money on something, why not the best? It does not occur to her yet that the best costs more or that she may not be able to afford it.

The family moves in for good on the 10th. For a few days Kim is busy rearranging, floating on the notion of her first American home. Quang goes to work, riding with one of the carpenters who lives nearby. I register the girls for school. And Kim, alone now in her house, goes into a slump from which she has yet to emerge— dramatic, immediate and draining for us all. Is it culture shock, catching up with her at last? The girls were at their lowest right around Labor Day and now have revived. And Quang, forced to go out every day to work, seems to have avoided it best of all.

I think in retrospect perhaps I should have been prepared; perhaps there was more I could do, now that we have been through it with Minh and Lan. One morning in late summer Kim and I went to the Board of Education for some English books and the foreign student director, seeing Kim, said watch out for culture shock—fatigue,

35

lassitude, nostalgia for the old country, unwillingness to participate. I thought nothing of it then, until soon Minh and Lan began to seem all too fond of their babysitting chores. They had been in the house almost all the time while Kim and I went out collecting things after the newspaper article. Now Minh, asked to go with us to the grocery, insisted she'd rather stay behind to watch the children. Lan, indifferent to food, stayed home while the rest of us went out one night for pizza. Soon Minh was also avoiding saying even the simplest words in English. The effort seemed to drain her. We teased, trying to shake her out of it. Ben announced that Vietnamese was forbidden in the house between six and eight in the evening. "What?" he would say when he heard Minh ask in Vietnamese for something at the dinner table. "I didn't understand that. Try again." And he made such a great joke of it that Minh began to ask for rice and iced tea in English.

But going out was something else. The jabber of English in the streets, the stares of Americans, Minh and Lan wanted none of it. On Labor Day weekend we finally convinced them to ride with us to the mall, to help look for Lisa's shoes. "The mall is like Saigon," Ben said. "Lots of people milling around the stores." They went, but when we got there they must have seen only the difference between this and home. After one quick foray through the center aisle, Minh and Lan retreated to the car, where we found them when we returned an hour later. They were sitting close to each other in the center of the back seat, windows closed in spite of the temperature. Too many strange sights for them, too much loud talk in a strange tongue.

And then, just as we were becoming really concerned, sudden cure. At the Lutheran church they started English lessons two nights a week with a private volunteer tutor, and Lan met another Vietnamese girl named Nguyen Brewer, a year younger than she is and in the same high school district. Nguyen hadn't surfaced during the rash of phone calls after the newspaper article because she isn't a refugee. With her Vietnamese mother, she has been here a year, come to live near her American father's family. Whether her father was killed in the war or her parents divorced, we don't know. Nguyen quickly replaced the girlfriend Lan missed so much from Indiantown Gap. And the next night the two girls went to a church supper with the refugee high school boy who lives with the Berings. They returned looking chipper enough to tackle anything. Their world was not to be populated entirely by English-speaking Americans after all.

Seizing their good humor, we registered the girls for school as soon as they settled into the apartment. This had been a source of concern to us for weeks. School had started. The school officials had been anything but receptive about taking them. Oh yes, they said, they would devise a program, they would call us back as soon as the rush of the first few days was over...but they never called. Crestville is no melting pot for immigrants; they hadn't the vaguest idea what to do with them. We pictured the girls being dumped into regular classes, ignored, retreating further into themselves—going once and then, in their gloomy frame of mind, refusing to go back just as they were refusing to leave the house. So when they seemed to be able to handle it at last, we enrolled them, Minh in the junior high and Lan in the high school, which was reluctant to take her until I suggested they put her in the same classes with Nguyen, who could translate for her. The guidance counselor, hearing that, was enormously relieved. All they need now is an English tutor.

And in fact going to school has seemed to be good for them. The girls go out every day, they hear English; living among Americans becomes part of their routine. The greatest problem so far has been explaining to Minh that because she lives within walking distance of the school, she really has no choice but to walk. The first morning, wearing uncomfortable shoes, she rubbed a blister on the back of her foot. "Tomorrow," she announced when she came home, "I no walk. I take bus." My explanations fell on unwilling ears, but we bought a pair of walking shoes with a gift certificate someone had sent, and the problem was solved.

In the meantime, Kim has been sitting at home, moping. Just as she seemed to thrive before the move when she was out every day with me, now in her isolation she is miserable. "The girls, they happy," Quang tells us. "But Kim, she cry all the time." There in the apartment she has nothing to do but talk to her refugee friends, dwell on her loneliness. Though I do the best I can, I get over there only about three times a week to rescue her, and even then it's a strain. I bring her here to do laundry (there are no facilities in the building, and she's too shy yet for the laundromat); I take her to run errands—the bank, the post office, the grocery store. But going takes planning. I am never there enough. Back in the summer, no one had to be anywhere at any special time, and Minh and Lan were available to watch the children. Now we're into our fall routine: a maze of activities and no such thing as a babysitter before 3:30 in the afternoon when the high school girls come home. Mike goes to nursery school three days a week from 9 to

11:30, Lisa must be rushed home to get on the kindergarten bus at 12. After lunch, Steve and Mike both sleep. At 3:15, Lisa arrives home. And though I may be imagining it, I feel that Kim blames me when I don't go to her apartment anyway, that she feels I am not taking care of her.

I try to show her she doesn't need me so constantly, that she can begin to do some of the errands herself, but she shies away. At the bank downtown, three blocks from the house, she knows how to make a deposit or write a check; at the A&P two blocks away, she knows the routine of buying groceries. But she will have none of it alone. She is afraid of being stranded with only her English. How can I blame her? But I do. I feel she is using me. I want her to leave me alone.

I try other things. I am desperate for Kim to establish a life of her own. One of her phone friends, a woman named Van, lives almost within walking distance, just off the bus route. I take her there while I run my own errands, hoping the visit will cheer her up enough that she will make it a regular thing, that she will go back herself. Van lives with her two preschool children in a second-floor apartment, much smaller than Kim's. Her husband, Trinh, works for an engineering firm in Jonesville, about ten miles away, leaving her more or less stranded. I think Kim will see this and be suddenly struck by the fact of her own mobility—all she has to do is get out and walk, get out and step on a bus—but she's as thick as pudding. She comes away looking as if she feels worse than ever. Who knows what they have said to each other? A week passes, and now two. Kim has made no attempt to go back, to go *anywhere*. Quang takes the bus to work on the morning his ride is tied up, but Kim, though she knows the routes and the mechanics, is afraid. Either I hold her hand and take her everywhere or she remains at home, glued to her phone. Ben says two weeks is not a very long time. But to me, feeling responsible for her, it has seemed an eternity. When I sit down to read or visit friends, I feel guilty. I have done almost no writing, except in this journal, since the family arrived. The time I would normally spend writing goes to these endless errands. What is more annoying yet is that for the past year and a half I have always found time to write in spite of the children, though they are demanding and have the more legitimate claim to me. But Kim, for some reason, stops me cold. Guilt: her sadness makes me feel as if I have no right to my own life. You take on these projects determined to make good no matter what; you hate to see the graceful gesture boil down to a residue of resentment. It isn't her fault I don't write. But I resent her for it all the same.

So now, this week, I have come up with a new idea. I hope it works. Stephanie, the director of Mike's nursery school, has been looking for help. The nursery school is less than two blocks from Kim's apartment. I ask Stephanie if Kim can be an aide. She hems and haws for a while, mumbling about the language barrier. Finally she says she'll try her out without pay if Kim agrees, to see how it works. If all goes well, there may be a salary later. Kim consents at once, and has started this week. I'm optimistic because though it's only three mornings, still it gets her out of the house, hearing English...and even if there's never a salary, it will be a good reference for later, when her English improves enough that she can look for a real job. Besides, the work seems especially well suited to her. Like Minh and Lan, Kim has that cheerful, accepting way with children. She often speaks of missing her niece, her sister's daughter, and I think when she is caring for children she forgets about herself for a while. Even Stephanie has said how much the students like her.

But here is the puzzle: three mornings of work and already Kim has missed one of them, without calling. I have asked her what the problem is, but she is vague. She says she likes the work, that she was sick. I wonder. I tell her it is important to keep commitments once you make them; I speak of the possibility of pay later, of job references. I tell her if she is going to miss a day, at least to call. (Whose welfare is really at stake here? Hers? Or mine? I hate to stick my neck out for somebody and then have them not show. And I hate to have her sitting at home, waiting for me to entertain her. What a complicated mess this is becoming!) We are beginning to be afraid that jobs, like so many other things, are a source of confusion to Kim and Quang, that all we are saying about their starting at the bottom until their English improves and working their way up is lost in some unfathomable difference of mind-set. Even Quang, who shows up every day for work, has stopped improving all too soon, and fallen into his own kind of rut.

Here is Quang now, five weeks into his stay here, able to read a tape measure and swing a hammer and distinguish between a 2x4 and a 2x6. Ben hopes to move him from labor onto a framing crew soon. It would make him feel that this training session has paid off. At the very least he wants to count on Quang for certain tasks. But now it becomes apparent that he can't. Quang nails a board down so that it is structurally sound but so rough-looking that no customer would accept it. When a job site has to be cleaned, Quang picks up some of the trash and most of the boards and lets the rest of it lay, apparently oblivious to what he hasn't been trained to see.

"In Vietnam people would be delighted to have a house like the ones we build," Ben says, "even with a few chips out of the woodwork or things lying on the floor at settlement. But *Americans* aren't going to accept that. Americans have such high standards that you have to do everything almost perfectly."

Again we are back to the difference between the huts with thatched roofs and mud floors, and our own wall-to-wall carpeting and electric stoves. How can Quang know what Americans expect when even the worst of it looks as good to him as anything he's ever seen? He will just have to learn, Ben says. He has to be around it for a while, and he will learn.

But oh the lesson. Someone starts to paint a downspout. Quitting time comes. The next day Quang has to finish it. Ben returns. The original paint had been brown; Quang has completed the job in white. "I *know* what he's thinking," Ben says. "He's thinking of paint from a protective standpoint and not an aesthetic one. Paint is paint, never mind what color it is. Any color will keep the metal from rusting. But *no* American would ever do that."

When they are on a tight schedule trying to ready a house for settlement, Ben becomes nervous. He never knows quite what Quang is going to do and then has to wait for him to do it over and, sometimes, over again. In the building business, appearances are so important. No matter that Quang is not doing finish work. Even the rough carpentry has to look good or the customers, unschooled in technical details, will think the work is shoddy. Cleanup is just as critical. The walls must be smooth and the carpets vacuumed and there must be no workmen's fingerprints on the paint.

My immediate reaction to all this is amusement. I imagine the two-tone downspout; I imagine some customer's astonishment. The lesson here seems to be for us too: it's hard to keep your sense of humor when you're paying for the joke by the hour. Poor Ben.

"To Quang's credit," he says, "He does whatever he's told. He never complains. But he does it so half-*assed*."

FIVE

Two months into her new life in America, and here is Kim these days: the skin on her face pale and spongy, hands cold as ice. Even her hair has lost its sheen and hangs limp as if she has not the energy to wash it. Until this week I didn't know if it was culture shock or illness...or how to distinguish which. I only half cared. I am so sick of all this.

Now I find the situation is even more complicated than I had guessed. For one thing, the family has not understood that we really mean what we say about self-sufficiency. They think only that we do not understand what they want; otherwise we would get it for them. We are the sugar-daddy Americans, putty in the right hands. So they tell us what they think will please, as if by playing us right they will make us provide. It isn't even gold-digging; it's simply the way they think things are. But aside from this misunderstanding about our roles, Kim has been struggling with something of which I knew nothing, apparently in the mistaken notion that to tell me would make me angry with her. So much has our confusion deepened.

At first it was mostly a matter of the job. Kim was showing up only sporadically, sometimes one day a week, sometimes two. Did she like the work? I would ask. Yes. If she didn't she had only to say so, to quit altogether. Oh no, the job was fine. Then why did she stay away?

"This morning tired," she would say.

"Sometimes Ben is tired in the morning too. But still he goes to work." There were a thousand excuses: her tiredness, the heat. A windstorm that cut the power lines. The rain.

Stephanie, the director, likes Kim and thought she was sick. "She's awfully pale," she would say when I went to pick up Mike, and so I would key on that. "Does your throat hurt?" I asked Kim. "Yes." "Your stomach?" "Sometimes." "Your head?" "Yes." Ah, explanation! The flu. Then Kim would pronounce herself better and appear for several days in a row before the absences began again.

41

And now, wary of my disapproval, she would call...not herself, but through her friend and interpreter, Yen. Like Minh a month ago, Kim found speaking in English to Stepanie suddenly too wearing. Ungracious, I suspected her motive was less culture shock or shyness than simple conviction that letting Yen talk to Stephanie would cushion the consequences. And soon Kim began relying on Yen to deal with me as well, every chance she could. No matter that except in times of illness we had done well enough without an interpreter before. "Oh," Kim says in her small voice now, pretending not to understand something I have said. "I call my friend." And I end up talking to Yen, who aside from the issue at hand always has a few words about the job. Kim is not feeling well, it is hard for her to get up. And then to the point: "Can't you get her a *paying* job?" I explain that Kim's lack of English makes it difficult, that the nursery school means not only a job reference but exposure to the language as well. If she dislikes it, she doesn't have to go. Though no one says this, I begin to feel that Kim thinks she is doing me a favor by going to the nursery school, instead of the other way around. And still she goes, one day a week perhaps, pale and cold as stone. Has money already become such a problem? Or is it only that she sees now we will not get her the color TV; she will have to buy it herself. Perhaps she feels that at the very least we could provide her a job to help pay for it.

But it is not only the job. It is errands too. We have gone beyond my showing Kim what to do and hoping she will do it next time. She simply won't. And if I don't understand, then she will play her game of manners with me, anything to get where she wants to go without resorting to the bus. In the car on the way here to do laundry, she perks up as if she has forgotten something and says suddenly, in the quavering voice I have come to think of as her beggar-voice, "Oh! I need....You know," and she licks the tip of her finger and puts it to her palm to show me: stamps. So we stop at the post office, with Steve and Lisa getting restless in the back of the car, and then continue on toward the house until we near the grocery store, at which point she perks up again and remembers something else—red pepper, perhaps—which she insists they do not have at the A&P near her house. How can I say no when we are already right there?

By the time we get home, Lisa is irritable and Steve howling and I am not much better. All this because of Kim's sad face. She clings to me as if I will keep her from drowning. I have gotten so I avoid going over, because I know we can never get to our destination in one stop.

Yen makes it worse. When I speak to her on the phone, she invents a few more errands I could run. Won't I take Kim to the health department to get a flu shot? No. We don't get the shots ourselves. Sometimes they are worse than the illness.

Yen has borrowed a Vietnamese-English dictionary for the family from the library. It is due back tomorrow. Since I will be at the apartment anyway, won't I return it for them? Yen has no driver's license and her husband will not be available until the weekend. No, I will not return the book, but I will take Kim there so she can return it herself. She should learn to use the library. Then I am angry. I had not meant to go to the library this week; I have other things to do. The library is five blocks from Kim's apartment, on the same street. Why can't she walk there herself or send the girls after school? But I go, and resent it.

It is not just shyness that makes Kim cling so, Ben and I decide. Yen, who has been here four years, condones the errand-running; she adds to it. And after all this time, how can *Yen* be shy? "In Vietnam," Ben says, "hardly anybody has a car. And anyone who does has the leisure to use it. They don't have much over there, but one thing they do have is time. They think you have it, too." In Saigon Kim walked to the market every morning; here she goes with me once a week. In Saigon she scrubbed her laundry by hand. Here my washing machine tumbles it clean while we talk. When she is here, she never sees me writing, and the children are often asleep. With all my chores taken care of, what else have I to do but take her where she wants to go? So goes Ben's reasoning. But still I thought she saw our hectic schedule, the children running in and out, needing to be taken here and there.

I am periodically ready to quit. Ben is horrified. Giving up just isn't *done*. He rides on the conviction that all things are possible, given enough effort. He believes that whatever you decide to do (no matter how useless, no matter how foolish), you give it your all. I am beginning to wonder why I went along with this harebrained scheme. For all that Ben has to deal with Quang's unreliability at work, his normal schedule hasn't been upset at all. Mine hasn't been the same for two solid months.

We begin to see another source of friction. At home, Kim is spending more and more time on the phone, talking to other refugees, comparing notes. All the other refugees are being sponsored by churches, which take care of them, which pay their rent. No one asks them to try to do things for themselves yet. And Kim, bewildered, thinks we owe it to her to do the same. I remember back to the first week of September, when I took Minh and Lan to the Berings' house to go to a church supper with the high school boy there, and I think I didn't like the church's attitude any better face to face than I do in theory.

It is a big old ramshackle house, not what I expected, full of worn furniture and a general air of decay. Mrs. Bering comes to the door to greet us, a baby on her hip. Her husband says a quick hello and then draws back. Three other children come in and out shyly, to get a look at us. The refugee family—husband, wife, high-school-aged brother, a baby—are living on the third floor, and have been for more than a month. Only the high-school boy comes down, to meet the girls. We do not see the others. The man, Mrs. Bering tells me, is working. The wife stays home. "They're saving for an apartment and a car later," she says. Later? Next month? Two months? "Well, we'll see how they do."

Mrs. Bering talks about her refugee family with genuine affection, but she seems tired, too, and I wonder how long she can go on cooking for five extra people before it wears her out. It is hard to take on strangers so completely, with no end in sight.

"But there are committees for everything," she tells me. "If they have to go to the doctor, or to language class, someone usually picks them up."

Someone. Usually. The small hard knot of activists, and the others who do nothing. We speak of the other refugees in town, Kim's telephone friends. One family lives in a tenant house belonging to a widow active in one of the churches—free rent in exchange for some housework and some farm chores. Van and Trinh—the couple with the two little children—live in an apartment in town. Someone goes there every day, to take Van on her errands. Someone babysits. Everything is provided for. But who will do it in six months? Is it kindness to provide everything until exhaustion sets in? Isn't it better to teach realities from the beginning? We think so. But for now, in all of Crestville, only Kim and Quang are minimally on their own. Does Kim resent it? Does she use Yen to ask for things she cannot get herself? It turns out that that is part of it, and only part.

Yen begins to apply more pressure yet. This time the target is Medicaid. Why won't I get Kim a medical card? The girls have them. Most of the other refugees in town have them. She names a list, a new tactic. So and so has food stamps, so and so gets money from welfare, the church is giving this one that. Why not Kim and Quang? I explain, but I admit the family's confusion is not unfounded. Already we have had two dental emergencies, coming within a week of each other. Minh and Quang have both developed abcesses; they have each had to have a molar pulled. Our dentist, familiar with the family from the newspaper, makes no charge for these initial visits. He wants to give us time to see how they will handle their expenses. Minh, he tells us, has a mouthful of cavities. We suspect that Lan does, too. Even in Saigon, dental services must have been poor.

Much as Ben dislikes government welfare programs, we decide to apply for Medicaid for Minh and Lan. Quang is not their father. Under ordinary circumstances he would not be supporting them at all. Would it be fair to expect him to handle their dental expenses on his laborer's salary? If he pays for his own medical work, and Kim's, that will give him an idea of how things are done in America. He should not have to pay for the girls too. But now, with the refugees talking back and forth to each other about what they are getting, Kim seems to feel Medicaid just for the girls is not enough. We explain that Quang probably makes too much money to be eligible for Medicaid for himself, though we have not checked into the details. Kim says nothing more. Now it is Yen who nags, though why she has picked this particular program as the center of her campaign, we don't understand at first.

"Yen doesn't realize what life is like for most Americans. She doesn't understand much better than Kim," Ben says. "Yen's husband is in the army. They don't pay for medical expenses; they just go to the base hospital and let the doctors take care of them. From what she sees, the role of the government is to provide all the services anyone needs. Now we come along and ask Kim and Quang to live off the economy. Apparently in Vietnam Kim and Quang never realized they would have to do that...and now here's their one friend who's been here for any length of time, the one person they think they can trust, who knows what's going on, and she isn't living off the economy either."

But surely Yen knows that some people pay? After four years, how can she have no inkling? We go back and forth, Yen listing the refugees and the programs that are taking care of them. "We're asking them to adopt a whole new value system," Ben says. "To Yen it *does* look as if we're only trying to make life harder for Kim and Quang. Of course it seems cruel."

One day I take Kim to see a refugee woman who lives in Henderson, a village just east of town. With her husband and two-year-old son, the woman, Nga, is living in the old parsonage there. Spence and Mary Tighe, the pastor and his wife, have recently moved into a newer place next door. Nga stays home with her son while her husband, O, works for the Board of Education. They speak very good English. He is helping to set up a program for the Vietnamese students in the county.

This is not entirely a social visit. A woman from Planned Parenthood has called us several times, a crusader, trying to get birth control information to all the refugees. "Otherwise," she says, "they seem to drop babies like flies." I dislike the analogy, but the principle seems sound. It can't hurt to have Kim learn about the Pill. Nga is to be her source of information. One of Planned Parenthood's success stories, Nga is on the Pill herself.

So for half an hour or so the two women, who have not met, seem to be having a pleasant visit, while I play with Nga's little boy, trying to be inconspicuous. Suddenly Kim bursts into tears. She sobs for a while, then wipes her eyes, becomes composed. For all Kim's sadness these past weeks and Quang's talk of her crying, I have never seen her in tears, or even close to it. The two women are embarrassed. I, an outsider, have intruded on a private moment. I ask Nga what is wrong. Nga mumbles something about Kim missing her country. It is possible. Nga is also from Saigon; they may have been reminiscing, but I think not. I have the feeling something more is bothering Kim, something immediate and specific. Then the moment passes; we talk of other things and I learn no more.

Ben thinks I am foolish for not believing Nga. "There are probably things going on in their minds that we can't even begin to imagine," he says. "How would you feel if you got out, knowing you were secure here and your family was still over there, and that you might never hear from them again? You wouldn't be happy. You'd feel too guilty to allow yourself to be happy. At least I would."

But while there is something to that, in this case it turns out that I am right. Kim's problem turns out to be specific indeed, and the visit to Nga holds special irony. Kim falls back into the old routine: going to the nursery school once, then having Yen call in sick. When I question her about it, she looks so uncomfortable that I stop. She comes here to do her laundry. Uneasy, she runs upstairs to fold whatever comes out of the dryer, then spends her time talking to her refugee friends on the phone, avoiding me. Once I come upon her unexpectedly, sitting wanly on the couch, not folding things with her usual burst of energy. She looks very ill. When she calls Yen, I say I want to talk. I ask Yen directly what is wrong.

"She can't eat," Yen says. "She can't hold much food on her stomach. She think she pregnant." She has missed one period already, and she has been nauseous ever since. The crying episode at Nga's house was brought on by the irony of being told about birth control just now, when her morning sickness is everpresent.

"She can't cook," Yen tells me. "It make her sick. She come to my house and I make her Vietnamese food she like."

More chitchat. My immediate reaction is anger, always anger. Why wasn't I told? Why was I left to make excuses for Kim at the nursery school...maybe she has the flu, maybe a stomach virus, maybe this or that? I say nothing, but I feel surer than ever that Kim has been going all this time because she thinks I want her to. It is not the Vietnamese way ever to say no. She has been doing me a favor, showing her good breeding, probably against the advice of Yen, who thinks she should be paid. And now I am being told because they need my help.

"Maybe you take her to doctor," Yen says, and I recognize in her tone the same small pleading sound Kim uses when she wants something, the beggar-voice. "Maybe get her some medicine for her stomach." As if without the pleading, I would not. It turns out Yen has a whole plan of action devised. The health department runs a free maternity clinic. Since Kim has no Medicaid, Yen wants her to go there so she won't have to pay. The problem is that a private physician has to refer her. I have three children of my own: maybe I can take Kim to my obstetrician to have her pregnancy confirmed? I can, of course. I make an appointment for her at the end of the month. I am to be her driver, her go-between. Yen is apparently to rule her life, no matter that we—her sponsors—are the ones asking favors from the community, putting our reputations on the line.

And then sometimes I close my eyes and conjure up my old image of the stereotyped American—the small-town suburban-house smugness, the roll of fat at the waist, the mind steeped in the Puritan ethic like a pickle in brine. How removed I've always felt from all that. I don't feel particularly American at all. My vision is too clear to let me believe people are poor because they don't work hard enough, too clear to let me wave flags and give ten dollars to the Heart Fund and feel comfortable about it. I think most city people feel this way. Then I learn Kim is pregnant and my first reaction is anger. Kim is twenty years old, sick, halfway across the world from the only home she knew until six months ago. And I am angry because I am not the first to be told. The stereotyped American is *me*.

With the secret out, Kim abandons the nursery school altogether, stays in the apartment, talks on the phone. Her sickness is with her all the time. "I no eat rice now," she tells me. "I eat fruit."

One morning the woman's director from the YMCA calls me to ask if Kim will help babysit there, for minimum wage. The Y provides babysitters in the mornings so women members can go to exercise classes. The job is only for two hours, on a day when the regular sitter cannot come. I go to Kim's apartment to talk to her about it. At once she calls Yen.

"Is this another volunteer job?" Yen asks sharply.

"No. It pays minimum wage." In that case, Yen says, Kim wants to do it.

"I don't care whether she takes the job or not," I tell her. "But if she says yes, then she has to stick to her word. If she's afraid she'll be too sick to go, it's better to refuse." I don't want Kim to feel pressured, but I want her to understand how serious a commitment is.

For a long moment Kim speaks rapidly in Vietnamese to Yen. Then she hands the phone to me.

"She say she can always sit for a short time with children," Yen tells me. "Even if she feel sick."

My anger comes flooding back. This job is no harder and not much different from the one at the nursery school, except for the pay. Yen has been hostile from the first to our letting Kim work for nothing. Our motives for getting her the nursery school job will never be understood. It does no good to speak of references, of learning the language. Yen understands only money, only direct, concrete favors done on Kim's behalf. And Kim doesn't understand, either. She's caught in the middle between my advice and Yen's.

"If you want them to understand you, you've got to be more direct," Ben tells me. "You can't try to be subtle, you can't beat the Vietnamese at their own game." Small comfort. At this moment I would like to tell Yen exactly what I think, but I'm afraid directness will mean throwing good manners out entirely. They seem to be all that saves us.

In the midst of all this gloom is only one rosy thing. Catholic

Charities has found Kim's cousin, Fon. He is at Ft. Chaffee, a resettlement camp in Arkansas. They are processing his papers so he can join Kim and Quang. Kim has a great need to see her family reunited. This will be the first step. He will arrive in a few days and the idea, in spite of everything, makes her happy.

SIX

Now Fon has arrived, has been here a month, this smiling, shuffling cousin of Kim's in his tight jeans and high-heeled shoes, who makes Kim and Quang, for all the difficulties we are having, seem the essence of unspoiled innocence. Even before he got here, Fon enclosed a note to us in a letter he wrote to Kim, blessing us three or four times for sponsoring him and announcing that, "I will do my best to become a good citizen of the most civilized and free country in the world." A little thick, we thought...but this was before we knew.

"At least he's smart enough to figure out what people want to hear," Ben said. "The Vietnamese love to tell you what you want to hear." After Kim and the nursery school job she loved so much, this was a little unsettling. We tried hard to reserve judgment.

Then Ben drove Kim and Quang to National Airport to pick up Fon the night he was to arrive, while I stayed home with the children. Ben returned less than enthusiastic. Fon stepped off the plane dressed to the teeth in mod clothes—high shoes, denim jacket, wide belt—and proceeded to bless and flatter Ben nonstop all the way home.

"Every third reference was to how God would bless us for taking him in," Ben told me. "That might work with those church people, but not with me." That same week a young man Ben dislikes showed up at the building site to apply for a job. Ben turned him down. The next day he showed up again, Bible in hand to demonstrate his good character. Ben sent him away. He soon learned the young man had been staying at the Rescue Mission, taking their free room and board for weeks. "Playing those guys for all they were worth," Ben says. Fon—like a Vietnamese version of the same young man—hardly soothes his nerves.

"Saigon Cowboy," Ben pronounces him. "That's what we called the smoking, doping kids who hung around the streets."

"Maybe not," I say. "Maybe he's just nervous meeting you."

"Let's hope so."

But Ben is right: Fon is hardly ultra-responsible. A few days after his arrival, Ben rearranges his whole work schedule so he can take Fon to the unemployment office to begin looking for a job. He is to pick Fon up at 1:00. At the last minute he is detained by a customer. Quang calls to explain to Fon that Ben will be a half-hour late. When Ben arrives at the apartment, no one is home. Some painters working outside say he has just gone off with a tall thin man in a red car. Ben is furious. It is difficult for him to get away from the site, and whatever else Fon may be doing, it cannot be as important as looking for work.

That night, Yen calls, ready with an excuse. Fon was in the base- ment, she tells Ben, and didn't hear the door. This is supposed to placate, because Ben has made clear that, until Fon is working, he should earn his keep by helping Quang pack up the trash. The trash is turning out to be more of a job than Stevens, the landlord, indicated. The people are supposed to bag it in plastic before they throw it down the chute. They don't. They take their garbage pails and empty them loose. Quang has the job of unclogging whatever gets stuck in the chute, then bagging it so he can take it outside. Fon has nothing else to do. At least he can ease Quang's work load. But would he be sorting trash when he was dressed for a job interview? And what about the man in the red car? How much does Yen think we will believe? I am half pleased to see Ben as irritated with Yen as I usually am when I hang up the phone.

The next day there is a downpour; the men at the site cannot work. Ben drives Quang home and confronts Fon face to face. Fon tells him he is sorry; he half admits that he went off with a friend. He pledges never to do it again.

"I felt like I was back in Vietnam," Ben says when he gets home. "The Vietnamese would smile and apologize all over the place, tell you what you wanted to hear and then do what they wanted to do, regardless. That's one reason we fared so badly over there." He says he will keep the pressure on Fon, make him understand he expects a return on his promises, not just empty, polite utterings.

A few days later Ben rearranges his schedule again. This time Fon is waiting for him. They go to the unemployment office. They have to wait more than an hour before they are called by an interviewer, who refuses to look either Ben or Fon directly in the eye. Fon did some sort of mechanical work in Vietnam, on airplanes, but he will take anything he can get here that doesn't require much English. The interviewer flips through a pile of index cards and announces that he sees no immediate possibilities. Ben's whole afternoon is wasted. He thinks the interviewer's function could have been served equally well by a bulletin board. His distaste for government programs is reinforced. He is determined to find Fon a job through private channels. Not long afterward his friend, Art Foreman, who plays in the "Y" basketball league with him, says a job as a dishwasher is open at one of the Coffee Cup restaurants he manages. Art is willing to give Fon a chance.

"You said you were worried about your future," Ben tells Fon, rehashing some of Fon's own rhetoric. "Well, here's your one chance—no second chance. You'd better arrive early and leave late if you want to move up."

Anxious to please, Fon works without incident for a week. Most days the job runs 3 to 11, with dinner included. Now that Kim is sick so much of the time, Minh is cooking for the family. Lan, who dislikes household chores, does nothing. With Fon away through the dinner hour, some of the pressure is off. And now that he is working, he will be able to start paying rent.

But as it turns out, Fon does not pay rent, at least not willingly. Ben has suggested Fon pay at least $25 a week for room and board; $35 would be better. Fon gets his first paycheck but fails to mention it to Quang. A bag from Sweeney's Shoe Store appears in his room—the Florsheim and Naturalizer dealer, nothing under $25. Ben asks Quang if Fon has paid him anything. Quang is vague. Fon has borrowed $15 from Quang to tide him over—money Quang sorely needs back. When Ben sees Fon, he explains again that Fon must pay his debts, the $15 owed, plus rent. Since he has no choice with Ben standing there, Fon pays.

Fon quickly acquires a set of inseparable friends, most of them bearded young men, generally unemployed. One is a 20-year-old named Kenny with long stringy unwashed hair, who spends most of his time at the apartment. Fon describes him to us glowingly as a student at the junior college, something he thinks will sit well. When I meet Kenny I ask him what classes he is taking. "Oh no," he says dreamily, looking at me through glazed eyes. "I'm out of school. I work part-time in a little grocery store." Then he falls quiet, staring at an English grammar book as if it is too much of an effort to speak.

One night the trash chute jams again, for the third or fourth time. Ben goes over to see what the problem is. He tells Quang he will call

Stevens, to have him remind the tenants again to bag their trash. When the two of them go upstairs from the basement, the whole front of the apartment is bathed in the sweet mist of marijuana coming from Fon's room. Strategically, Fon has managed to slip out to the store.

"What worries me is who's supplying whom," Ben says. "I can understand him seeking out the friends because he's lonely, but I can't understand the reverse. He may be only buying something, but he damn well better not be selling it."

The friends begin to be everpresent in the apartment, whether Fon is there or not. Kim, as a Vietnamese more hospitable than we are, cannot bring herself to ask them to leave. One day I have to pick Kim up in early afternoon. Minh has arrived home from school but Lan has not. Two sleazy young men are sitting in the family room, waiting for Fon. Kim and I move to go, but the friends continue to sit; they plan to stay. Suddenly I am afraid for Minh being there alone with them.

"Does Minh want to go with us?" I ask, but Kim shakes her head. Lan will be there soon. I think Kim would rather have both girls in the apartment together than either of them there separately. I want to say something but remember it is not my apartment, or my place. Later I reconsider; I should have asked the boys to go. My American upbringing allows me to be blunt. Kim would have forgiven my rudeness.

One night Fon's friendliness gets him in deeper than he means to go. At 3:30 in the morning our phone rings. It is Fon, asking Ben for Quang's number. Can it be that he has forgotten? It is his own number, too. What is going on? He is spending the night at a friend's house down near the river, he says. Ben mumbles his way through the conversation, half asleep. Then, suddenly wide awake, he spends the rest of the night worrying. Why the call? And how can Fon possibly get to work by 10 a.m. the next day, to work the early shift for which he is scheduled? Somehow he does. He hitchikes home, changes his clothes and goes right to the restaurant.

Two days later, Fon finds himself alone with Ben and Quang, and explains. "I call to ask for help," he says, though unless Ben is mistaken he never quite got around to it. He does a pantomime of how a "boy-girl" picked him up while he was walking home from work, and whisked him off to his house by the river. "That night," Fon says, "I no sleep. I fall asleep, then..." He runs his fingers up and down Quang's chest to demonstrate and puckers up his lips. "Give kiss, give kiss."

"No like, no like, I say," Fon yells, jumping back. At last, at 3:30, he calls Ben for help, in a code which Ben cannot decipher. Finally he uses a screwdriver to unlatch the door, while his host is asleep, and sneaks stealthily away.

Ben cannot help being amused. Fon is a good storyteller. But also thinks Fon is often too drugged to know what he is doing. Ben becomes more and more angry. He has Quang bring Fon out to the site to talk to him. Ben has a sheet of drywall in his hands. He uses it to write some of the words down, so everything is clear. Marijuana is illegal in this country, Ben tells Fon, along with a whole slew of other drugs. Normally he doesn't care whether people smoke it or not, but he doesn't want it in the apartment with Minh and Lan. He doesn't want it where it could be discovered, and put the whole family in jeopardy. He wants no trouble with the police. He warns of danger, of legal action, of deportation. Fon goes into his now familiar act. He apologizes, promises not to do it again. Then he plays for sympathy.

"I am all alone," he says. "I want to go back to my country." There have been newspaper articles about 1,500 refugees who went back to Vietnam on a freighter from Guam. Both Ben and Fon know it was a one-time thing, but Fon means to use it. Annoyed, Ben says that is fine with him. "In fact if I ever see or smell or hear of any drugs in that apartment again, I'll personally put you in a rowboat and let you paddle back." It begins to dawn on Fon that Ben is serious: he expects more than lip service to promises. Fon starts to do his smoking and doping elsewhere. Only the friends remain as much in evidence as ever.

Some of the friends are women. Two young men and two women come to dinner once a week. About these Quang does not complain, though he can ill afford to feed them. What worries Quang is the much older woman who stayed a good part of the night one time, and the prostitute he saw Fon pay just before she left. Quang, too, is concerned about the impression Fon makes on the girls.

Knowing this, Fon's latest ploy, whenever Ben puts any pressure on him, is to announce he plans to assume his rightful place as head of the family.

"In Vietnam," he says, "Minh and Lan no follow brother-in-law. They follow cousin."

"I wouldn't mind your wanting to have an honored place in the family if you were responsible," Ben tells him. "But being responsible means supporting the whole family, not just yourself, and thinking of their welfare."

To this Fon is usually vague. He never pays rent unless Ben speaks of it specifically. He would rather spend his money on clothes. When Vikki, from the Indochinese Task Force, takes him to choose from a clothing bank set up at one of the churches, he sneers at most of it, taking only one winter jacket now that it's getting cold. No second-hand castoffs for Fon; he wants only shoes from Sweeney's, the best. But at Quang's expense?

And Kim and Quang seem to be paralyzed in this matter by their sense of tradition. Fon is an honored guest; therefore he can stay for as long as he likes, whatever it costs them, no matter how much they need the money themselves. Instead of confronting Fon, they begin to complain about their poverty to their English tutors. Mrs. Carson, the director of the language school, calls us and asks what is wrong. Isn't some welfare help in order? Can't we get them food stamps? She reminds us of Yen, without the Vietnamese accent. How do we explain that this is a war of manners going on here, more than of finances? We don't. Ben becomes impatient with the church people and their easy sympathy. "It's one thing to listen to somebody cry poor," he says. "It's another to go down to the welfare department and get something for them." And of course it's true. They love to pay lip service to Quang's plight, but they are not so willing to take action on his behalf. They seem to see their role as policemen of sorts, except that they usually hear only one fragment of the story before they quickly call it to our attention, righteous with indignation.

Ben decides that if Quang is going to be head of his family, he will have to act the part. He will have to collect Fon's rent. When Ben asks if he has, Quang shakes his head sadly and says, "Too much friends." The apartment has been too full of people; Quang has not been able to talk to Fon alone. Quang seems to have lost control. The friends rule the apartment. Uncomfortable at handling what should be a purely internal problem, Ben collects the rent himself. And as if to retaliate, Fon talks again about the girls. He will be their leader, he says. Maybe he will take them back to Vietnam.

If this is designed to annoy, it does. Though there's no chance of a return to Vietnam, still the girls have just gotten over the worst of their homesickness. They are doing well in school and speaking a little more English. Why does he have to remind them?

"To be the leader you have to set a good example," Ben tells Fon. "Work hard, no drugs, all the rest."

"But I am first cousin," Fon argues.

"You're not in Vietnam anymore, pal," says Ben in disgust.

The only bright side is that so far the girls seem to take Fon lightly. They let him stomp around importantly and then go about their business.

And yet Fon's behavior takes its toll. On the night of the autumn parade, which goes directly in front of Quang's apartment, Fon and the friends go out onto the sidewalk where the crowd is gathered, carrying whiskey bottles and being quite loud. Friends of ours who are across the street, who have met Quang once and are unaware of Fon, think Quang is the rabble-rouser. "I didn't *think* that could have been him," they say when we explain, "acting like that." But we sense that their doubts remain. If Fon carries on so, and if he's a member of the family, who knows what the others are like?

A month of Fon; it seems like years. This week he almost got fired. One of the other dishwashers brought whiskey into the back of the restaurant one night just before quitting time. Everyone got drunk, Fon included. We've heard two versions: that they got drunk while they were still working, and that they didn't start drinking until after. One of the men was fired. Fon wasn't, out of courtesy to us. No second chance, Ben told him, but it looks like he is getting one all the same.

SEVEN

Maybe I should be grateful that Fon is here. Otherwise Kim and I would have no issue at all on which to agree. First it was the stories about what was wrong when she discovered she was pregnant...and the errands. Now it is more errands still, and crying poor to all the Americans they meet, especially their English teachers. On the one hand they seem not to trust us at all; on the other they are ready to have us do everything for them, to cling to us as if they were children.

"There is a Chinese grocery store in Holiday Acres," Kim has Yen tell me in her beggar-voice. "You know?"

"Mmmnn."

"Kim, she like the rice they sell there. She can buy it in big bags, not cost too much. Maybe you take her there one day?"

"I don't think I have time. Why don't *you* take her there on the weekend when your husband is home?" This tactic, I have learned—shifting the burden to Yen herself—always renders her quiet. Some of the Vietnamese families in town have begun to buy cars. We think this is a good sign and that they will be able to carpool with each other now. I must explain my position to Kim more clearly, Ben says. It might look simple enough for me to get in the car and take her here and there, but really it isn't. I have three children to care for, work to do, friends to see. "If you want to say no, *say* it," Ben says. "It's the Vietnamese custom to say yes all the time, not an American one." I try, but the message does not sink in quickly. Though the Vietnamese families now have the capability to help Kim, still it is us she turns to for help.

She has become close to a woman named Ha, who lives with her husband and two children in a farm tenant house owned by a member of one of the churches, a lady named Mrs. Sievers. Ha is pregnant with a third child, hence the special bond between her and Kim. The family pays no rent. Instead, Ha does Mrs. Siever's housework and her husband, Tu, does farm chores on weekends. Since Tu works in a factory where pay is good, they have been able to buy a secondhand car. Now Ha has offered Kim a bicycle, which she wants Ben to pick up. We are unsure why we have been accorded this honor. One night Ben comes in early while Kim is still at our house doing laundry. He is going to take Quang to a new English class that is being offered at the CETA store-front building, in addition to the classes at the church. He decides to run Kim home and, on the way, pick up the bicycle, since there are about 15 minutes to spare and Kim has said Ha lives in Pikeview, only a mile away. They arrive in Pikeview.

"Where is your bicycle?" asks Ben. "Show me the house."

"There," Kim tells him, pointing to a road leading out into the country.

"How far?"

"I don't know."

"Tell me in time how far," Ben says. "One minute? Ten minutes?"

"Maybe five minutes."

"It's too late," Ben tells her, tapping his watch. "Quang has to be at his class." He turns the car around and heads toward Kim's apartment. Theory into action: when it is inconvenient to run the errands, don't do it.

"Doesn't Ha's husband have a car?" Ben asks.

"Yes," says Kim.

"Do you go out sometimes in your friend's car?"

Yes again.

"Then why didn't your friend bring the bicycle to your house?"

"Too many people in car," says Kim. "Two families."

"But the bike doesn't go in the car. It goes in the trunk."

"Too many people in car," says Kim.

I don't know, too many people, the blank look Kim gives when she would prefer not to understand...these are the catch-words now. Anything to achieve the desired ends. Even Ben, who is endlessly patient compared to me, is sometimes becoming annoyed. I do admire his ability to act according to his principles. He manages to map out his position in his mind beforehand, so that when Kim's errand takes too long he has no qualms about refusing her. He doesn't go anyway, as I often do, and then come home fuming. He's also more consistent than I am, a virtue you're supposed to develop with children, and probably also useful with refugees. I, on the other hand, find myself swayed equally by my philosophical position and the mood of the day. If Kim seems especially down, if I am especially up, I will do more for her (or less, depending) than I intended. Only lately, knowing what is coming, have I grown less flexible.

So now, seeing this, Kim is turning to others more and more, especially her English teachers. The latest thing, with the weather turning cold, is that she has told her teacher she and her family need coats.

But how can it be? Back in August the girls each got a coat from the Indo-Chinese Task Force collection. Someone brought over a heavy army jacket for Quang. Other coats came in through the newspaper article. Surely they have enough. Nevertheless, alerted by the English tutor, Vikki Anderson from the Task Force takes the family to the clothing collection again, where each chooses another coat. A ploy to get sympathy, I think. Ben says no. "They hear too much about how cold it is here. *They* don't know. They think you need a different coat every day of the week." Little by little the trust chips away. Did they really think we'd let them freeze?

On the last day of October, I take Kim to my obstetrician, Dr. Banks, to have her pregnancy confirmed so he can refer her to the free clinic. To our surprise, Dr. Banks offers to see Kim for the rest of her pregnancy, without charge.

"If she goes to the clinic, she'll see a different medical student every time, and with her language problem it's going to be awfully difficult. I decided that I'd sooner have the refugees come to the office. If there are funds to pay the bill, fine. If not...." He waves his hands in the air. I am reminded of the unassuming kindness we have run into so often from individuals...the dentist, some of the people who donated household goods, and now the doctor. Only the public agencies—the interviewer from the unemployment service with his shifty eyes, the counselors at the high school who were so reluctant to take Lan—try to demean them as much as they can.

But the situation with Dr. Banks presents us with a new problem. How to explain to Kim and Quang that they don't *have* to pay him anything, but should? We speak of self-respect, of pride. Paying five dollars is better than paying nothing. Most of the $1,200 subsidy money still sits in the bank in a savings account. It would not be impossible to offer something in thanks. But as they did when we went to the Rescue Mission for furniture, Kim and Quang ignore our advice. The clinic is free. If the doctor is also free, then so be it. I know they will never pay him a penny. I am disgusted, but do I yell and scream and stamp my feet? No indeed, at least not in the presence of Kim. I stomp around the house and tell Ben I've had enough. Let them fend for themselves from now on. This is our scenario: I threaten to quit almost weekly; Ben calms me down. At work Quang is poking around, too unreliable with hammer and nails, physically too weak to carry drywall, oblivious to the trash that has to be cleared from the site. But Ben, stubborn, wouldn't dream of quitting. "You just have to keep kicking ass and taking names." I stop sputtering, grit my teeth and prepare for another day. A good thing too. A few days later the obstetrician's generosity is forgotten. Kim, far from being grateful, complains to her English teacher about her financial plight.

"Quang, he no work when it rain," she tells the teacher. "We no have money to buy food. Maybe you get me a job? I make more money to buy food?"

Shaken when the teacher tells her this, Mrs. Carson calls me up at once. Always it is Mrs. Carson who calls, the school's director, or else Vikki Anderson from the Task Force. The family has no money? The family is about to starve? No, no, there is still about $1,000 in subsidy money in the bank; the situation is not as dire as it seems.

Ah, says Mrs. Carson, as if she suddenly remembers. "When Nguyen Brewer's mother came here last year, she was the same way. We were breaking our necks trying to get her settled and she was complaining to everyone that no one was helping her."

If that is so, why is she so quick to assign the blame to us? But still she is suspicious.

"Is it true Quang doesn't get paid when it rains?"

"When there's no indoor work to do. That doesn't happen very often." Besides, Fon has an income now; if he pays his rent, there is money coming in regardless.

"Most of the families have food stamps, you know."

"We think Quang makes too much money to be eligible," I tell her. "Of course if you want to look into it yourself...."

"Oh no, that's all right." Suddenly the family's situation seems more equitable. Mrs. Carson and Vikki Anderson are always telling us that something should be done; they are never anxious to *do* it. As for the job, Mrs. Carson says, with Kim being pregnant and unable to work after June, there's not much she can do. We hang up, problem resolved. I sit by the telephone and fume.

"If they're going to tell everyone we're starving them and freezing them, why help them at all? Whatever we do it isn't going to be good enough."

This evening Ben has a new theory ready to test. We never know how much gets lost in translation, he says. When Kim tells someone she needs money to buy food, she may not mean that literally; it is only her way of making clear that she wants a job. We must give the family the benefit of the doubt.

But I am not so sure. "Ellen," Kim says the next time I see her—in the unmistakable beggar-voice, "you think maybe I can get food stamps for Minh and Lan? Not for Quang and me, just Minh and Lan." I shrug, looking skeptical. Kim goes on with her case. "My friend, Ha, you know her? Her husband work, but still she get food stamps for her children."

This one gets, that one gets; when the language teachers won't get it for her she turns back to us, confused, feeling deprived. The great American wealth is out there somewhere, but elusive.

"Ben and I don't think you need food stamps," I tell her. "If you want them, you will have to get someone else to see about them for you, or do it yourself."

"Oh," Kim says in a small voice. And we do not hear about food stamps again.

Another week passes. Vikki Anderson from the Task Force calls. Is it true, she wants to know, that while Kim will not have to pay for her doctor, she will have to pay her hospital bills? This is what Quang has been telling his English teacher. Can it be true that Quang has no Medicaid? No medical insurance? How can it be that he will have to pay?

"Listen," I say, as angry and self-righteous as she is. "We don't think Quang is eligible for Medicaid and we don't believe he needs it even if he is. We're afraid that once he gets on the public dole it'll be too comfortable there for him ever to want to get off it. If you people think it's such a good thing, why don't you send one of your volunteers with him down to the welfare department? Ben doesn't have a big company or a large cash flow. He doesn't have an office, just a construction trailer, and he has exactly five men working for him, four of them single and not at all interested in medical insurance. Besides, even if he did offer insurance, Quang wouldn't get it free for his whole family. He'd have to pay for it. And there's no guarantee he'd get maternity benefits even then. Kim got pregnant something like three weeks after they got here. I don't see you telling Quang *that*."

My anger gives Vikki pause. She backs down. I tell her the truth: that we have been trying to explain to Quang what the situation really is, so that he will have some basis for coping with life in America on his own. If he is not eligible for Medicaid, as we suspect (and we are going to go no further than suspicions; if he wants to apply for it, he will have to do it himself), then he has no choice but to pay his hospital bill, a few dollars a month if necessary. We've done it ourselves and know it is not so impossible.

"Right after Steve was born," I tell her, "our older son, Mike, had to have eye surgery. By the time we got finished we had both the maternity bill and Mike's surgical bill hanging over us. The only insurance we carried was major medical, which paid something like $40 towards the eye operation. For the rest of it we sent in whatever we could each month, and gradually it's getting paid. We've told Quang he can do the same thing. Why should you tell him he doesn't have to go that route, when in the end he may have to whether he likes it or not? It's nice to think that because he's a refugee we ought to make things easier for him, but beyond a certain point they aren't going to be. Why is it so hard for you people to recognize that?"

Vikki is silent. Having spent my anger on the do-gooders, my fury remains for Kim and Quang. I write Kim a long note, so that nothing will get lost in translation. It is one thing to be poor; another to make yourself out poorer than you are. For emergencies, the subsidy money sits in the bank. If Fon pays his rent, even emergencies should be affordable.

If Kim really wants a job, she must work on her English. Nothing comes easy. It is not a matter of somone *getting* her a job. It is a matter of working long enough and hard enough on her language that she becomes qualified to *do* a job. I am tired of hearing "I don't know" whenever she would rather not answer a question. In America there is nothing wrong with saying what you think; it is more wrong to say what the other person would like to hear, what will bring the desired reaction, when it has nothing to do with reality. Straightforward as it is, the note sounds more polite than I feel. I am tired of bringing Kim here to do laundry; I am tired of taking her to the store; I am tired of her refusal to do for herself, her crybaby tactics. Her morning sickness is gradually passing now. It is no longer a valid excuse. Ben and I expected to help the family until they could get on their feet. They are *on* their feet, if only they would recognize it. But they seem not to see it. They expect us to provide more. Whatever is given, it is not enough. Taking charity is not to be a short-term necessity, it is to be a way of life.

But not for Minh and Lan. One of the first things they brought home from school were slips to fill out for free lunches if the family made below a certain income level. They refused even to consider it. Not for them looking poor in front of their peers. They would rather go without lunch...especially Lan, who rarely eats lunch anyway. If only Kim and Quang would learn something from them about pride.

Kim and I go to the drugstore to fill a prescription for her nausea pills. The druggist hands us the bottle; Kim opens her purse and shows me. No money. I have no choice but to pay. I tell her this is a loan; she must pay me back. It is not that I mind paying for necessities like medicine if she really needs help. I think, though, that this is not poverty, it is strategy. I have no wish to be like the rich uncle, doling out coins at Tet. Seeing that I am serious, the next time we meet Kim pays me at once. Unlike Fon, she is sensitive, she is responsible. It is only that we play out our battle of wills.

Thanksgiving comes. An old man who lives at the YMCA has befriended the family. He brings them a turkey, sweet potatoes, a pumpkin pie. They come to our house on Thursday but on Friday, with the old man's help, Kim cooks a Thanksgiving meal of her own. "Why do they take all that?" I ask Ben. "They're probably telling him they don't have enough money for food, either."

"He's just an old man without any friends. He can afford the turkey, and they don't mind having him over. It's a good deal for everybody." I must temper my judgment. It is easy to mistake for begging what to Kim is only good manners, only hospitality. One reason the Vietnamese get so much is that they accept it with such good grace.

At Thanksgiving dinner we ask Kim and Quang if Fon is paying rent now. They look at each other and reply, almost with one voice, "I think so." Now that my note has put "I don't know" off limits, "I think so" is to become the new party line. It is hard not to be amused. How difficult, if you have been trained all your life not to say what will displease, to change completely in a few months for the sake of a few willful Americans.

One day we are in the grocery store, just as my tolerance for taking Kim marketing has almost given way. We go up to the meat counter and I discover she does indeed need help. The things she wants are not always on display—pork heart, brains, other variety meats. And she does not know how to describe them in English.

Some days the tension melts. We sit in my family room on a golden late-fall afternoon. Kim does not insist on calling Yen to translate. She is glad to be here. Now that the heat is on in her apartment, the gas fumes from the furnace rise into their rooms and bother her stomach. She tells me about Lan. Even in Saigon Lan would try to get out of household chores, although there it was not so easy. "I come in, my head hurt, I say get me Coca," Kim tells me, using the standard word for Coca-Cola. "Lan no want to, but I am big sister. She no can say no." Now, away from her father, away from the traditional family hierarchy, she is more stubborn. "I tell Lan she no cook, no eat," Kim says, "and she say okay. She no eat." Instead of becoming angry, Kim laughs at Lan's bullheadedness. For her, it is the way of life to accept people as they are...even Lan, who makes life harder for her, even Fon with his sleazy friends, even me, I suppose. With all our disagreements, once I say no to a particular request, the subject is always dropped. There is never an outward grudge. Kim is always smiling, always courteous. And on these rare afternoons we still talk.

"In my country," she tells me, "The houses...very close." She puts her palms together to show me, then points to our large yard and the neighbor's house next door. My neighbor, home during the summer, has now gone to work. Kim notices this and finds it a source of sadness. "In my country," she says, "you talk to her *every* day. If you go away, she watch your children." There are no babysitters; it would never occur to anyone to get one. She speaks of her father, of Fon. At home Fon was very bad. She motions to show me how her father beat him; she laughs. She speaks of her large family, the neighbors, the maiden aunts she visited in the summer at Tam Ky, of a crowded friendly life. I feel guilty for wishing she would talk less on the phone to her refugee friends, comparing what each has gotten. I realize the friends are all she has, and I feel guilty for her loneliness, which I do so little to relieve. I wish to explain the cold, private nature of some Americans, like me. I cannot. Some of our days together are still golden.

And on others the contest between us is muted; we are almost on the same side. The nurse in Dr. Banks' office wishes to get a history. "I call my friend?" Kim asks of Yen. I tell her no. She must not always rely on Yen to translate; she must learn to deal with Americans herself.

So instead *I* become the interpreter. The nurse asks her questions in English to me; I ask them in English to Kim. Any history of heart trouble? "Heart. You know, Kim. Here." I pound my chest, making pumping motions with my fist. Kim looks blank. Any history of diabetes? Liver disorders? It is too ridiculous. We laugh. Always other Americans speak to us, to Ben and me, as if when we repeat it it will be somehow easier for Kim and Quang to understand. "Maybe you'd better write the questions down," I say to the nurse. "We'll come back next time with the answers." One round for Yen. Sometimes an interpreter is essential.

And then Mrs. Carson calls again, with another question about the family's well-being. We have squared off soundly now, church against state, liberal against conservative. The English tutors are all sympathy, telling the family what they should have.

"If somebody comes to you with a problem, it's only human nature to want to sympathize and help him with it," Ben says. "It's harder to say no, you don't have a problem after all, it's just something you have to live with. What these people don't realize is that they're teaching the refugees to be very skilled at *getting*. Not at earning, just getting." So Kim and Quang polish their sob stories and try them out over and over again on the theory that the more Americans they can get to sympathize with their plight, the more potential handouts. So far it's worked up to a point...and now that it isn't working so well, when their practical experience no longer backs up their belief that the mother lode is there to tap, they only become frustrated and lean on us harder. Not only that, but the more shocked disbelief they see over their situation, the worse they themselves think it is, the more removed from the average American lifestyle.

And the church people have no respect for our intention to stand on our position as firmly as they do on theirs. We think food stamps and welfare checks are traps. If they believe so firmly that they are salvation, why don't they help the family get them? When it comes right down to it, they don't seem to have the time to help Kim and Quang fill out the forms...only to call us and berate us for not doing it ourselves.

So here we are, the season of peace on earth and goodwill toward men approaching, wishing some of the tutors or the Task Force people or anyone other than us would once in a while stop telling Kim and Quang what they ought to "get" and tell them the truth. Everyone has bills, budgeting is hard, there is no free lunch except in the public schools—and then if you take it you are automatically set apart from everyone else as an object of scorn.

EIGHT

For two months it seems that relationships have been shifting and changing but that when we look back at them nothing has really been clarified and we understand each other no better than ever. If there has been a change, it has been a tiny one, in the Americans. There seems to be a crack in the do-gooders' armor.

Back in the middle of December Minh received a letter from a girlfriend, addressed to her in care of us. It seems another letter, which got lost, had been sent earlier. A message on the outside of the envelope asked us to make sure this one didn't suffer the same fate: "To the sponsors of the Vietnamese family," it read: "Can you bring this letter for them and the letter I send before. If you forgot, you can bring it for them right now. If you can't, you can phone for them. Thank you very much for your helping and praise the Lord heaven to you." So typical, it seems. The refugees don't much trust us or think we're very bright, but they feel it's easy to manipulate us by touching our soft spots...in this case, religion. Even Fon kept up his blessings and references to God for weeks when he first got here, until he discovered Ben wasn't a church-goer. Then (again to please?) he told Ben he wasn't very religious himself and started on his poor lonely alien act as a replacement. I wonder how the Berings or the Carsons or Vikki Anderson would take to Fon, or to this letter for that matter. The refugees are handled by so many religious groups, sponsored by so many churches, that they think we will be spurred into action by the merest religious reference. And if not, then there must be something else....

So still there is this constant probing and testing, to see what it will be...just when I, for one, am beginning to feel harder. By mid-December Kim's health has returned. I am trying to get my Christmas shopping done, I am doing some writing. I am busy. Ben says when I don't want to do something, don't do it. I call Kim less. I think she is confused about the bank, doesn't understand that the drive-in window in the suburbs and the main branch downtown, near her apartment, are part of one and the same. I take her there once, twice. I show her. Then I go no more. I shop alone. I tell her to walk to the post office. I think maybe she will have no choice: she will have to go herself. I have underestimated her desire to depend.

Kim does not strike out on her own. She does not start asking for favors from her Vietnamese friends. Instead she makes another American "friend," a woman named Patti Winter, her new benefactor, who does for her all the things I have refused. I don't know where Kim found her. I discover her only when Patti starts to call occasionally, when she cannot understand something Kim is trying to tell her. Kim does laundry at her house, Patti says, and she shops with her once a week at the supermarket. Patti drives her to the Chinese grocery in Holiday Park now and then. "I feel so sorry for her," Patti says...and I have learned enough not to protest. On Thursdays, Fon's day off, Fon spends the day at Patti's house, talking to her husband, Jim, who works the late shift. Jim picks him up; Fon brings a six-pack. How long this has been going on is not clear. A month, perhaps, by the time I hear about it. Already they have grown a bit weary of Fon. And in mid-December Patti calls me, confused. Kim has asked her for a color TV.

"She looked at ours and said, 'Can you get me this?'" Patti tells me. "She really thought we might have an extra one."

"Someone gave them a black-and-white TV when they first got here," I say. "We think she doesn't realize what a big difference there is in cost."

"Maybe," says Patti doubtfully.

The incident is embarrassing. I feel like a mother who has failed to teach her children good manners. The next time I see Kim I tell her outright that this is not something she can ask for. "You save money and buy a color TV yourself," I say. Kim looks at me but seems deliberately vague. Perhaps she doesn't really believe buying one is the only answer; perhaps she thinks I am only trying to make life more difficult for her again. I know she still has little capacity for assessing the relative value of American goods. To her it must seem as if every American has everything, that nothing can be very hard to get—for Americans. But she has been spending her own money long enough that I expect her to begin to see the difference, to understand that a color TV costs less than a car but more than a black-and-white TV or the cheap record player someone gave her when they first

moved in. Once or twice at the mall I have watched her price difference pieces of jewelry with Quang. I think they are trying to figure out
what her opal ring is worth...and I can't believe they haven't priced
other things they are interested in too. Even if not, we have talked
about the color TV before. Do they think everyone has an extra $500
to spend on one—or at least every American, everyone but the
refugees? And that if we won't get it for her—or Patti won't—it is
because we simply don't want to out of selfishness?

Another time Patti calls because there has been a misunderstanding with Fon. Fon has told Jim Winter about his dissatisfaction with
his job, which is so different from the mechanic's work he did in the
Vietnamese Air Force before he came here. Jim has said he knows
someone who may have an opening for a mechanic in a garage. Fon
takes this as a promise. He speaks of it constantly, to Jim and also to
Ben. The job turns out not to materialize. Fon is disppointed. The
other kitchen help no longer work well with him, and he is on the
verge of being dismissed from the restaurant.

"Prejudice," Ben says on Fon's behalf. "Not incompetence." But
Fon insists he doesn't care, one way or the other. He doesn't want to
work as a dishwasher. "I want to work with my mind," he tells Ben,
pronouncing the word with a short *i*.

"If you want to work with your mind, you'd better do something to
improve your English first," Ben says.

Fon looks down, points to an empty wooden chair in the room. "I
am like that," he says. "All alone." On the one hand, Ben knows it is
more or less true. Fon has failed to take his place as king of the roost
at home.

"On the other hand," Ben tells me, "I almost told him I wished he
were alone a little more, without the friends. I managed to restrain
myself."

In spite of Ben's admonitions, Fon does not improve at home. He
does not pay rent, he does not help with the trash or the furnace. He
puts cigarettes out in the house plants and leaves beer cans on the
floor. Subtly, without saying so outright, Quang hints that the family
would be better off without him. Kim, intent on becoming the center
of an extended family here just as her father was at home, is remarkably pliable.

"I know he no good," Kim tells us, though we are not sure what she
means by the term "no good." "Still I want him to live here if he
happy. But he no is happy." Taking this as tacit consent, Ben calls

Catholic Charities in Baltimore, suggesting Fon might want to leave. Catholic Charities sends a young man up to counsel him. The young man tells him of English classes and other government programs, things Fon already knows, as if the problem were that he were being given too little instead of taking too much. Fon insists he is content. The young man leaves with the notion that Fon needed only some extra personal attention, thinking everything is resolved.

Now Stevens becomes increasingly impatient, first with Fon and then with the rest of the family. He does not like the stream of friends wandering in and out of the apartment; he is displeased with Quang's handling of the furnace and the trash. Once or twice Ben goes over to the apartment so he and Quang and Stevens can all go through the routine as Stevens wishes it done. The furnace is achingly old. Ben thinks the problems are more of age than of Quang's inability to stoke it properly. As for the trash, is is still not being bagged by the tenants; it is still three times the job it ought to be. But Ben is afraid Quang is as careless about the trash as he is about details at work...and that Stevens sees the few pieces of newspaper lying around, or the coal cinders, and notices how slowly Quang works, and draws the conclusion that he is handling the whole job poorly. Ben is always fighting this same line of reasoning himself.

"At work sometimes I look at Quang and think if he went any slower he'd be going backwards. I know it's partly because he paces himself. He's so much smaller than the other guys that he has to or he'd wear himself out. But when we see him moving around normally at home, he's like a different person." And what he does on the construction site does not quite explain the same attitude in the basement of the apartment house. Where Ben tries to understand, Stevens sees only that to Quang work is an endurance to be gotten through, however badly. He becomes more and more annoyed.

Finally he calls Ben one night with what we think is an excuse to get rid of the whole family. Fon has appropriated an old television set from the basement, Stevens tells him, which he has specifically said he couldn't have. One of the tenants has also seen Fon tinkering with the mailboxes. Quang's lease indicates four tenants. "And then you move the cousin in on me," he says. He is ready to evict them all. Ben promises we will get rid of Fon.

Again, Ben calls Catholic Charities, telling them firmly this time that Fon has to go. Before long they have located a family outside of Baltimore to take him. The week before Christmas, Fon is supposed to take the bus to the city, where the Catholic Charities people will meet him and take him to his new home.

"He's scheduled to go on Friday morning," Ben tells Quang. "Tell him I'll take him to the bus at 9:30.

Early Friday morning Kim calls. Fon has disappeared. Soon Art Foreman, the manager of the restaurant where Fon worked, tells us he has received a call from the Rescue Mission, which originally gave us most of Quang's furniture. Fon has thrown himself at the mercy of the Mission people; he has told them that he is being thrown out of town.

"I tried to explain to them," Art says, "and they sent him to the Red Cross."

The Red Cross, from Fon's point of view, turns out to be equally indifferent. From there he flees to Jim Winter's house. Jim calls us frantically, trying to locate Ben. He is convinced Ben has a personal vendetta against Fon and is trying to do him terrible harm.

Ben talks to Jim Winter for nearly half an hour, explaining. Ultimately Ben convinces him the move to Baltimore is for the best. Fon ends up at the bus station as planned, where Ben waits with him until the bus has actually departed.

For the moment Fon's departure takes the pressure off all of us. Kim's house is peaceful, if lonely. Finances ease. One afternoon Kim and I are driving home from the doctor's office, and Kim tells me again how her father used to have to be very stern with Fon. "Oh, he get angry too *much*," she says laughing, finding Fon very funny now that he is safely gone.

Just before Christmas I buy Kim one of the long red dresses she has been eyeing all these months, a present. She wears it to Ben's company Christmas party, looking radiant and healthy.

Then on Christmas night Fon turns up again. He is here, he says, only for a visit. His job hasn't started yet; he plans to stay for a week. On the second night he fills the apartment with friends. Quang, braver now that Fon is not a permanent guest, asks them to leave. They don't. Several of the friends go out on the sidewalk brandishing whiskey bottles and a blaring radio. They are arrested for disturbing the peace. Fon somehow escapes the same fate.

The next day, Fon declares he is sad again. He is living outside the city with a farmer. "I am all alone," he says. "I have no friends." Ben is sure that, without urging, he will never go back. Ben tells him he cannot stay: Stevens won't allow it. Even Quang tells him he must leave. Now that his own tenancy is on the line, Quang is not so hesitant about making his position known. That evening Fon takes off, this time without a scene. He tells the family he may go to Florida soon, or California. We wait uneasily, expecting him to reappear at any moment, but he doesn't.

As soon as Fon ceases to be a problem, we fall back into our own petty misunderstandings. On Christmas day I invite Kim's family for dinner, thinking they may have nowhere else to go. I also invite my parents and my sister's family, who come up from Washington. The table cannot easily seat everyone, but we make do. I buy a huge turkey, which barely gets done. Kim and Quang and the girls show up late. It turns out they have been to dinner just before at the home of Ha and Tu, their Vietnamese friends who live on the farm. They have even eaten at an odd hour so they can get to our house on time, so as not to disappoint us. The girls are too stuffed to eat. Quang tries valiantly to make the effort. We are swamped with leftovers. We wish they would tell us when they do not want to come; we really wouldn't have minded. It does not seem to be in them to say no.

We go to a holiday party at the home of our dentist, the one who treated Minh and Quang free when they both had abcesses during the same week. Now that Minh and Lan have their Medicaid cards, he is seeing them regularly, doing the work that needs to be done little by little. At the party we see other people who have worked with the refugees through their churches. One of them is a woman named Chris Flowers, who has been helping Van and Trinh, the family living not far from Kim. For the first time we detect a note of disillusion; for the first time the discontent is aimed at someone other than us.

"I was disappointed in them," Chris says, "because they would always say, 'We don't have this yet,' 'We don't have that yet,' as if we were expected to get it for them. Trinh has a good job."

Like Kim and Quang, Trinh and Van are convinced they are entitled to a great deal, through in this case Trinh's position as an engineering aide (his English is very good) earns him enough to be able to afford most of what he needs.

"He has a brother who's a student in France," Chris tells us. "His parents used to send him money from Vietnam, but now of course they can't, so Trinh is trying to help him. He asked us to get the brother a coat to send over there. His attitude is because I have this responsibility you have to help me that much more."

And their idea of help is often different from ours, Chris says.

"When they first got here I brought over a whole carload of clothes for the children, and Van sent them back. 'She don't like used things,' Trinh told us. 'She like new.'"

Now Van is about to go to work in a sewing factory in a neighboring town. Chris has all but lost interest in the family; she hears this only through others. For months Van has been waiting to get a job with the Yamaha dealer here. "But her English is almost nonexistent. She used to sell motorcycles in Vietnam, but how she expects to do it here without speaking the language...I guess this sewing thing means she's finally stopped dreaming."

We tell Chris of Fon. Fon, too, wants to work with his mind. Fon, too, likes only new clothes. Fon, too, expects.

And then, at New Year's, another chink in the American armor. Mrs. Sievers has asked Ha and Tu to leave the tenant house on her farm; the arrangement is not working out. In return for the house Ha is expected to do Mrs. Sievers housework—very difficult for her now, at the end of her pregnancy, with two preschoolers already underfoot—and Tu is expected to do farm chores. The trouble is that the farm work takes up most of Tu's weekend, the only time he has to visit with Vietnamese friends. For a month or two, neither the housework nor the chores have been getting done. Now Mrs. Sievers wants to rent the house to someone who will be more reliable. No one else in the sponsoring church is willing to offer shelter. So Ha and Tu have applied for public housing.

What distresses me is that Ha and Tu—and Kim as well—are so shocked at Mrs. Sievers' lack of charity. They see themselves as being kicked out, treated unfairly. But why? Vikki Anderson from the Task Force describes Mrs. Sievers as a middle-aged widow who's often sick and really needs the help. If Ha and Tu find the arrangement less than ideal, why shouldn't they bow out gracefully? Why should they expect to keep the house, for free, when they aren't living up to their end of the bargain? I think it all goes back to the same thing: the refugees expect more of us than we ever intended to give...and part of the reason they expect it is that we didn't set our limits very clearly. We didn't say that comfort always comes with a few conditions. To get free rent, housework. To get welfare, a salary below such-and-such. To get anything, some unpleasantness. Nothing is what it seems.

In a way, hearing these small stories that filter down to us, we cannot help but be relieved. We are only two people with limited finances, limited time. We have always known we couldn't give Kim and Quang everything. It is reassuring to know that even the churches, with their large charity collections and committees to run errands, are also capable of running out of steam. It doesn't ease things with Kim and Quang; it only makes us feel less inhuman. American charity is enthusiastic, but short-lived, even our own. It must be our initial enthusiasm that has given the refugee such high hopes; and now, as our concern with abstractions fades into having clothes returned because they are not good enough, as our patience dims—even the patience of the churches—Ben and I are no longer any more evil than the rest of them. For now anyway.

In mid-January the Task Force organizes a party to celebrate Tet, the Vietnamese New Year, as important a holiday to them as Christmas is to us. All the Vietnamese in town and all their sponsors, whole church congregations, are invited. The Vietnamese women prepare food—rice with shrimp and pork and slices of carrot, fried shrimp chips, vegetable molds—a huge table piled with traditional dishes. All morning Kim has run back and forth from her apartment, helping. The party is to be held at one of the churches across the street. She is wearing maternity clothes now, looking healthy. On the table, the *nuoc mam* is served discreetly to the side, to cater to American tastes. Kim urges us to try everything; she wants to make sure we are fed. She is concerned that we like the various dishes, which we do. She is the gracious hostess today, a role she plays well.

Ben asks Lan and Minh if they serve *nuoc mam* in the cafeteria at school. "*Nuoc mam* no is strong," Lan insists. It's the pepper and garlic some people put in it. We think the girls have become hardened to our teasing about their food, but they have not. They bring us this dish and that; they want us to accept. How much have we asked them to accept of our culture? Asked? Demanded. Today it is our turn to try to please. We eat too much; Minh and Lan beam.

But under the great show of Vietnamese-American solidarity, put on for local television cameras which later show us all on the 6:00 news, the tug-of-war goes on. We meet Ha and Tu, for the first time, and their two little children. Ha is hugely pregnant; we do not understand how she can move, much less do housework. We also meet Mrs. Sievers, a slow-moving, gray-haired woman. She had a mastectomy some years ago, Minh tells us, and often is in pain. "When she hurt, she scream at Ha," Minh says. "She very mean. Ha cry all the time."

Two sides to the story: an old woman, in pain, needing household help, willing to trade her tenant house for it; a refugee family slowed down by Ha's pregnancy, and wanting to visit friends on weekends. Their friends, the eight or so other refugee families in town, are all the link they have now to the old life. Tu does not want to give up his weekends for farm work. It is difficult for both sides. Is there a villain in the piece?

"Have they applied for public housing already?" Ben asks Kim.

"Yes. But they must wait long time. Maybe one year."

In the meantime, Mrs. Sievers moves through the crowd, talking to other people from her church, and Ha sings Vietnamese folk songs, accompanied by someone else's guitar. Each smiles at the other. The day is for public consumption only.

More chinks in the armor. Spence and Mary Tighe, the pastor and his wife from Henderson, are there with Nga and O, who live in the old parsonage next door. I have not seen Nga since the embarrassing day when Kim, newly pregnant, broke down crying in her house after hearing about birth control pills. "Is O still working for the Board of Education?" I ask Mary. Here at least is one success story. O's good English has gotten him this fine job setting up programs for the Vietnamese students. But O is between jobs now, Mary says vaguely. The Board of Education had too few Vietnamese students to warrant a special consultant. Nga is working though. "She's at the textile plant in Jonesburg," Mary tells us. "It's a union shop. The pay is very good."

"Then is O taking care of their little boy?"

"Oh no. A lady from the churches does that. O is looking for work."

The Berings are conspiciously absent from the party; so is the family they are sponsoring. The family is thinking of moving to California, someone says. So soon? There is much fond talk of California. California is warm, the colleges are free. Many Vietnamese have settled in California. And some few have gone to Baltimore, where there are also more Vietnamese; some have gone to Washington. A few have their eye on Texas. Under the smiles, under the clinking of dishes, the stirring of discontent. The churches grow tired of providing; the refugees, bewildered, are looking for bluer skies. Looking for work, looking for housing, all the neat arrangements beginning to give way.

A weekday now, and Quang is on the job at eight as always, even when Craig, the carpenter, and Ronny don't show up because of the bitter cold. Quang does whatever he is told; he never complains. He does it slowly, creeping through the day, as if in a daze where details blur into each other and lose their importance, as if still in a dirt-floored hut somewhere, where sweeping or not sweeping makes little difference in controlling the dust and the dirt.

A trim strip needs painting at the top of one of the houses, just under the roof. Quang sets up a high ladder, finds the can of stain, climbs up. The next morning Ben discovers that Quang has painted the whole strip except for a few inches below the top. Then he has gone on to other work.

"Craig or Ronny would probably bitch about having to get up on that ladder in the cold," Ben says. "But once they were up there they wouldn't get down again until the job was done right. Even if it were quitting time."

Re-education. Quang must set the ladder up again, get the stain, finish the job, in the hopes that eventually he will understand that doing it halfway only creates more work, that it is easier to do it correctly the first time.

"I bet he nearly froze," Ben says. "But what else am I supposed to do?"

Stevens calls, complaining about the furnace again. Quang cannot be doing the job correctly. Quang is not removing all the cinders. Quang must be putting in too much coal. Quang this, Quang that. What does Stevens know of rice paddies irrigated by hand, where a measure of efficiency one way or the other makes no difference at all? What does he care? Now, three months of furnace troubles later, he decides to convert the coal furnace to oil.

"Since he won't have all the work to do, I'm going to have to up the rent," he says. "It'll be $50 more a month from now on."

"Oh?" says Ben. "I don't remember the lease saying anything about the rent going up if you convert the furnace." Besides, Quang is still taking out the trash, which has always been more of a job than the furnace, what with the tenants neglecting to bag it and the chutes clogging. Stevens has apparently pulled this $50 number out of the air, another hope of getting the family to move. But seeing that he is likely to get no more money at all, he quickly backs down. Ben says he will think about it. At last he tells Stevens he thinks $20 more a month would be fair, this to placate, to insure that he does not invent more excuses to boot the family out. The latest in our soap opera now: we have told Kim and Quang they will have to pay this extra and have been met with stony acquiescence. Even they know how much better this apartment is than what most of their friends have, for the price. But the rumblings about finances have grown louder. We feel we might be sitting on a volcano that is about to erupt.

NINE

April 1976

In the middle of February, Kim's friend Ha had her baby, and suddenly the whole family—Ha, Tu, the two little boys and the baby—were living in Kim's apartment, for how long we had no idea. At first we thought they were staying just long enough for Ha to recover from the birth. I would ask Kim how long Ha would be there and she would say, "Maybe two weeks..." and I would think that was when the family would go back to the Sievers' farm, to await the public housing they have applied for.

Then, about the first of March, we learn that the move is not a visit. The family has made their break with Mrs. Sievers and plans to stay until the public housing comes through...whenever that is, a week, a month, a year. It seems that Ha has decided she cannot do Mrs. Sievers' housework and take care of an infant as well. Mrs. Sievers, in turn, has decided she has had enough of Tu visiting friends on weekends instead of taking care of the farm. She has rented her tenant house to someone else. Ha's family is told to leave. The sympathetic churchmen who are sponsoring Ha and Tu seem to have disappeared into the mists. The family is left homeless. Ignoring Stevens' rumblings over Fon and the furnace, Kim and Quang take them in. As we filter through what Kim has said to us, we realize she has been trying to make the situation clear. Much as we wish we'd understood beforehand, we cannot help admiring them. Hospitality is more important than the threat of eviction.

On a visit to the apartment, I find Ha's children napping in the darkened living room. Ha and the baby are using Fon's bedroom; Kim's family has the two back bedrooms. The family room and kitchen are shared. For all its size, the apartment is too small for nine, and Stevens seems not to have been forgotten after all. The atmosphere is deliberately hushed. Like children who sneak a puppy into school, they try to evade the teacher.

Can it be that the sponsoring church has really abandoned them to this? I call the church's pastor, asking him to explain. Oh no, he says, the move was planned. It is just temporary after all. Someone has been in touch with Stevens and gotten his permission for the family to stay for a while. (This, I soon discover, is not true, though the pastor seems to believe it. Too many cooks stirring the pot...and no one seems to know what the other has done.) The pastor is all complacency and friendly enough. He is not surprised by the conflict between Ha and Tu and Mrs. Sievers, he says. Several years ago he was involved with helping a Cambodian family, and they, too, became unhappy with what was being provided. "So we just let them drift for a while," he tells me. "Later they got on their feet and surprisingly there was no bitterness. They never held it against us." But much as I realize I have been letting Kim "drift," too, in my way, I wonder that he can let go so easily. Free rent and money to buy a car and food stamps...and now nothing. What would have happened if Kim and Quang had not been there to catch them when the church let go?

March, and the family is still living in, with no word from public housing. Kim tells Mrs. Carson again that she hasn't enough money to buy food, the same old story. Vikki from the Task Force calls with this comforting news: the Task Force is beginning to think Mrs. Carson enjoys stirring up trouble. Ben agrees. Mrs. Carson is inventing things. But is she? We ask Quang if Ha and Tu are paying rent, not becoming a drain like Fon. He tells us they are. After all the misunderstandings about Fon in the fall, can we expect him to tell us anything else? Money is tight. The regular babysitter at the "Y" has quit; Kim is sitting there regularly in the mornings now, but whatever she earns, it is not enough. Again we feel pushed into the middle. Hospitality is high on their priority list, and we admire them for putting themselves out so much for casual friends...but if Kim and Quang want to be hospitable, is it our responsibility to see that they can do it in comfort? Ben says no. This time it is to be an internal matter. They must collect rent from Tu or take the consequences. Quang must be head of his own house.

And as to food, Ha still has her food stamps. We think they are using them to buy at least part of what they eat. With the help of their sponsoring church, Ha and Tu have cashed in on all the government welfare programs and now, living there, have fired up Kim's own welfare campaign again. If the private benefactors will not come through, perhaps the government will provide for her after all. "We pay Mr. Stevens too much," she says. "I fill out forms for government apartment...like my friend." We say nothing. The wait for public housing may be long. Kim's is no emergency; she is not on the priority list. It is only that if they ever get in with neighbors who know the welfare game, we are afraid they will become permanently dependent on the government programs and never think of themselves as self-supporting. Better not to earn too much or try too hard, for fear the government help will be taken away. We see what has happened already with their exposure to Ha and Tu.

Only the girls are not ready to fling themselves at the government's mercy. Minh's junior high school counselor calls, saying Minh seems depressed. "She told one of her teachers they might have to move," the counselor says. "Maybe that's it—another upheaval." All these months Minh has learned English so quickly; her real personality seems to have emerged—bubbly, outgoing. Even more than Kim, she is the family extrovert. And now this. But the weeks drag by, with Ha and Tu still in residence at Kim's house, and Minh seems to recover. If Ha and Tu have to wait so long, perhaps her own family's move is not imminent after all.

And still it keeps coming, the strategies for getting more. Catholic Charities sends out a newsletter each month to the refugees and their sponsors. It tells of scholarships for the needy, free language programs, ways to avoid paying late penalties on electric bills...all well and good, even necessary sometimes, but not always or indefinitely or for everyone—a fact the newsletter fails to reveal. Having seen to food stamps and Medicaid, and having grown weary, even Ha's church withdraws without mentioning that being a refugee does not merit welfare in and of itself. And for all they've received, Ha and Tu are still novices at the game, not understanding that what was designed to prevent starvation will not also bring luxury. They hear of public housing, but none of the refugees here actually live in it yet. What do Ha and Tu imagine it will be like? Better than their tenant house in the country in exchange for some work?

The winter drags on, and the refugees begin to move around like pieces on a chess board, Ha to Kim's house, the Bering's family to California, two other families to Washington, Nga and O to Baltimore. What is happening? All the news we hear is bad. The Berings, grown tired of an extra family in their house, hint that it is time for the refugees to move on—but not three thousand miles away! Much as the refugees talk of friends in California, the church expects them to settle in Crestville, where the members can point and say, see, here are the people we have helped. We gave them everything and now they still come to church every Sunday, and see how well they are doing. Like grandparents, the Berings want to be able to show off their progeny. When it becomes clear the family plans to deny them this—for all the Berings have done, the refugees see their real friends as being on the West Coast—the relationship cools. The family leaves hastily, anxious to escape their discomfort. They have not been heard from since. I wonder how we would feel if Kim and Quang moved now? Hurt? Or relieved? Maybe a little of both.

Early spring, and the exodus gathers strength. Mary Tighe calls one day from Henderson to tell us the story of Nga and O.

"They're gone," she says. "To Baltimore, but no one knows their address."

This surprises me, even though I have known since the Tet party that the Board of Education had to let O go for lack of Vietnamese students. I imagined him finding something else right away, with his good English. The parsonage where he lived was so nice that I didn't think he would want to leave. And Nga's job in the textile plant paid well. Union jobs like that are hard to come by. Why would they decide to go?

"To his credit he looked for work for two months," Mary says. "But all he wanted was a management position and there just *wasn't* anything. So he more or less stopped looking."

Then the trouble began. The family had been paying only $40 a month rent for the house since spring; the church had been paying utilities. Now the finance committee began to be impatient. The house would normally rent for $250 a month; it was time for O to pay more rent or move on.

The woman who watched his son grew impatient, too. She didn't mind watching him, gratis, while O was looking for work, but if he was going to stay home, shouldn't he watch his son himself? Or pay her for the favor?

Nga and O seemed not to understand. So many friendly faces, such harmony all this time. The congregation has agreed to help until "later," until the family can support itself. Eight months have passed. They have taken the arrangement to be permanent. Trying to help, Spence finds O a job in a school kitchen, so they can meet their expenses.

"He went once," Mary tells me. "He came home saying it was

woman's work and that he wouldn't do it." O refuses to go back. Saving face is more important than earning money. He sees it as the church's responsibility to allow him his pride. Pressures build. What is pride if not self-respect, if not the ability to be self-supporting? It is not as if O is illiterate. He spoke fluent English even before he arrived. No longer a symbol of oppressed humanity, Nga and O begin to look less worthy of the congregation's charity than other causes. And yet this is really not what Nga and O had expected. They had really thought the parsonage was there for the taking, and the babysitter. It was part of the American way of life, the American wealth, was it not? They begin to feel trapped. The Americans are not what they seemed. The open hand has shut into a fist.

Searching frantically for a way out, O turns to a distant relative who lives in Baltimore. In Baltimore there are many refugees; he will not be left alone to deal with Americans and their confusing ways. He will be among people he understands. The uncle has promised to get him a $3.50 an hour job; O makes preparations to leave. Spence and Mary try to explain to him that in the city life will be more expensive. But now the trust is broken. O will not listen. "It costs less to live in Baltimore," he insists. "My uncle pays less, and there are no taxes there." "There are taxes everywhere," Spence says. O ignores him. Baltimore is the America he had expected. It is only Henderson that is different, out of step.

Not long before they leave, Nga decides to take a week's sick leave from her job, to go apartment hunting in Baltimore. Spence tells her she isn't sick and can't ethically take sick leave for the trip. Tempers flare. Who is he to dictate morals to her? Nga asks. She has ten days sick leave coming; she has joined the union and cannot lose her job. She seems genuinely to believe this. Mary and Spence try to clarify the union's function, but Nga refuses to listen. She thinks Spence is trying to make life more difficult for her, that he is being spiteful.

"We are leaving because the pastor no speak to us anymore," she tells everyone.

Before they go, Nga asks a neighbor to get her some furniture to take with her to Baltimore. "The things in the house here belong to the church," she says. By this time, Nga and O have over $1,000 of their own in savings. No one can understand why they are still asking for more. "No one would get them anything, of course," Mary says. "But to *expect*...." And yet, somehow, they do. They go in a huff, without furniture, thinking they have been betrayed. They do not leave their new address. In the parish, those left behind are also bitter. Such lack of gratitude. So many stories.

A good example, Ben says, of why we must always give Kim and Quang the benefit of the doubt whenever there is a misunderstanding. Too much gets jumbled otherwise. Who knows what Nga and O thought of the unions, of the wage scale in Baltimore? Who knows what information they are getting, and from whom, and what confusion there must be in their minds when they hear the stories from other misinformed refugees whom they trust? It is our obligation to be there for Kim and Quang, to listen and then make clear what our position is without getting angry. The church in Henderson left things too open, never setting up timetables, never reiterating that its support was intended as temporary—a babysitter for three months, rent subsidy for six—and that then the family would be expected to fend for itself. Or even, in harsher terms, that it was O's ability to support himself that was the church's interest, not his personal happiness in a job.

Nga and O spoke fluent English, Ben says, so part of the problem is not simply in the translation but the whole way of seeing things. Much as we try, we view life from different sides of the mirror. What seems clear and straightforward to us, with our American mind-set, must look quite different from Kim and Quang's Vietnamese point of view. Nga and O, seeing the church's affluence, may have thought it quite natural that the church should want to go on supporting them indefinitely. They may have been no more gold-diggers than Kim and Quang are, for all that they seem to want too much. They may have expected only what, were the situations reversed, they would have demanded of themselves. Look at Kim and Quang, what difficulties they endured for Fon, in the name of hospitality. And look at them now, living shoulder to shoulder with five casual friends, met only a few months before, again in the name of family and hospitality. In Vietnam there is little material wealth, but what there is is given freely. The meals may be meager and the rooms crowded, but no one begrudges the lack of privacy or the extra cooking, even if it goes on for months. And one more thing: in their culture, the receiver seems to have the same status as the giver. There is no shame to it. No wonder Nga and O have left in anger. No one told them about the American saying that old fish and guests should be thrown out after the third day.

So Ben says. But understanding makes the day-to-day living no easier and *do* we understand? One theory supplants another, but there is no telling whether we are right. I watch Kim's generosity with Ha and Tu and admire it, but for all the philosophizing, I find myself free with goods and money for only about a month at a stretch. Then I'm ready to pinch pennies. And I'm always stingy with my most precious commodity, my time.

In mid-March, Kim calls me to remind me the next day is her doctor's appointment. Usually I make the appointments and mark them on my calendar, but this time I must have forgotten. I have other plans and cannot take her. "But you can go yourself," I say. "You can take a taxi." Now taxis have become part of the public transportation issue. Kim lives in the center of town—a $2.00 ride to any place in the city, a bargain in an emergency...and while they're too expensive for everyday travelling, I've urged her to try a taxi once, so she'll know how just in case. We've gone over and over the mechanics of how it's done.

But Kim refuses to go alone, taxi or no. She convinces Patti Winter to give her a ride. As it turns out, it is lucky Patti is along. Kim had made a mistake about the appointment date. Perhaps that is why I didn't have it marked on my calendar. No matter, Patti arranges to have Kim seen anyway. At the end of the visit, a new twist. Kim is presented with the doctor's usual $300 bill. The receptionist is new and does not realize Kim is not paying. "You should begin to pay on this," the girl tells her, seeing how far along Kim is in her pregnancy. "By your next visit, you should definitely have put something down."

In Crestville, doctors' receptionists often act as bill-collecting agencies, trying to strongarm the patients into prompt payment. The usual procedure at Dr. Banks' office is to pay something each month, so that the bill is paid up by the time the baby is due. Thoroughly intimidated, Kim says nothing; she only puts the bill in her purse. Patti, who is aware of our arrangement, is nevertheless confused. Instead of confronting the receptionist, she waits until she gets home and calls me.

My reactions: anger and guilt. Anger at the receptionist for giving Kim a tongue-lashing, for not realizing that Kim, with her poor English, advanced pregnancy and obvious confusion, must have been a special case. Anger at Patti for ducking out as soon as the heat was on, leaving Kim in the lurch. Guilty for not taking Kim after all. Guilty for wanting my time to myself. Angry with Kim for not starting to deal with the doctor's office sooner, for leaving the job to me. Am I to be chauffeur in perpetuity? What else to do? Leave Kim with instructions to phone me as soon as things go wrong? I call the doctor's office and reap apologies, assurances that Kim will not be billed again.

By the next day when I speak to Kim, to explain that the mix-up has been put to rights, the incident has been blown out of all proportion. Kim, panicked by the prospect of having to pay the doctor after all, has called Yen, complaining about the new financial burden to be dumped into her lap. Yen has called the Task Force people; she has called Mrs. Carson from the language school; she has called everyone she can think of who may have some sway over Ben and me, who may get us back in line to fulfill our promises. (*Our* promises?) Yen tells me she has called the health department, trying again to get Kim referred to the free maternity clinic. Yen has apparently been on the phone nonstop since the afternoon before. And what am I going to do about it now? she demands. I tell her I care very little *where* Kim goes for her prenatal care, whether to Dr. Banks or to the clinic. I think, all things considered, it will be easier to continue with Dr. Banks, but the choice is up to her. Yen is somewhat taken aback by my nonchalance. All these months she has been dredging up the free clinic periodically, as if it were a threat to me, something I wish to avoid at all costs. Knowing how little Ben and I like government programs, she apparently believes we wish to keep Kim away from them (even their maternity clinics) with the fervor of parents trying to protect a daughter from an undesirable suitor.

Days go by, and the incident expands into ever-widening circles. Vikki from the Task Force calls, demanding to know if the story Mrs. Carson is telling is true. It seems I have told Kim she has to pay her doctor's bill after all. If she doesn't, I won't drive her to the office anymore. She will have to take a taxi. Like sentences whispered from one child to another down a long line, the stories become distorted, twisted. We have become the villains again.

TEN

May 1976

At the end of April, two long months after they moved in with Kim and Quang, Ha and Tu were finally notified that a place had opened up for them in the public housing project. Here is Ha's new home: a tiny two-story townhouse, built in the 40's, brick on the outside, the walls cinderblock on the interior. You walk directly into a living room, perhaps 12' x 12'. Behind that is a kitchen, just big enough to eat in. Upstairs, three tiny bedrooms. Behind the units are yards with clotheslines strung across. The grass grows only in patches along the edges. The play area is mud. For this Tu pays 25% of his salary. The rent includes utilities. The place is altogether about half the size of Kim's apartment. Since the move, we have heard less about Kim and Quang moving, and Minh seems cheerful enough again, back to her old self.

Now the thrust seems to be at finding some other way of easing their lot. Quang tells Ben he wants to get into framing, but Ben is skeptical because he does nothing to demonstrate his ambition.

"When I was in college working as a laborer," he says, "I'd dive for the hammer every free minute, until they began to depend on me. That's what you do. You know the guys with the hammers are the most important." But Quang never hustles; it seems not to be in him to do it. "He's typically Vietnamese," says Ben.

And what is typically Vietnamese? Uncomplaining, but also inefficient. Passive rather than aggressive, unassumingly nice. Mostly qualities desirable in a laborer rather than a framer, where daring and attention to detail count for something. Ronny, for all his coarse language, loves to balance on the second floor beams, and his finished work always looks *finished*.

Now Ben is trying a new tactic, hoping to bring Quang out. This spring he has begun to expand the company. His younger brother, Matthew, has recently arrived to work for him, an engineer like Ben though only one year out of college. Eventually Matthew will become project manager so Ben can rent a real office, in addition to the construction trailer, and spend more time on management. For now, Matthew is on a newly-created framing crew, learning how the houses are put together. With him is Craig—a good carpenter, brighter than Ronny and less vocal—and now Quang, their laborer. Perhaps Ronny's belligerence, his attitude that Quang (smaller, non-white, non-English-speaking) is therefore lesser—perhaps this is what is keeping Quang down. We will see.

Quang is different from Kim. Aside from his talk of going into framing, he asks for very little. He does what he is told; he never complains. It is Kim who rails against her fate. Is it because in Vietnam Quang's parents were farmers, while Kim's lived in the city, working for the government? Or because his family hadn't the pretensions Kim's had, and because he came here expecting less? Or perhaps, as Ben thinks, because Quang sees every day on the job that even the rich Americans exert effort for their rewards. Nothing comes easy.

"He sees how hard I work to get what I have," says Ben. "He sees that I'm there more hours than any of those guys and what I do." Most days, Ben swings a hammer with the rest of them. This is the problem, of course: there is too little time left over for management. But Quang sees that Ben takes his shirt off and gets dirty and is not above carrying drywall or digging ditches if necessary. Fon, when he was here, wanted to work with his mind...but Quang sees that even a rich man (relatively) can use his muscles until he gets tired. That is how he earns his money. "What does Kim see?" Ben asks. "Church people. English teachers who tell her about food stamps." And Kim sees, for the most part, American women who are a good ten years older than she is, who own their own homes and all the accoutrements to go with them. Quang, working with men his own age and younger, sees that his lifestyle is not appreciably different from theirs. He sees that most young people do not start at the top.

And though Quang is slow, though his work is often far below standard, still he seems to have a certain sense of perspective Kim lacks. Even at the beginning, when money began trickling in and Kim cast her eye on the clothing racks in the department stores, Quang seemed uncomfortable in the shops, wanting to get his family away from that rich array of goods...as if he understood that first things came first. Now if only he would learn to take some initiative himself, to experiment with a hammer, even—as Ben has been urging him—learn to drive. But he is still the child, too obedient, too willing to be led. Ben is convinced that in time he will change.

No easy spring, this. Kim, round but still pale, soon loses her main source of help. After the doctor's office episode, Patti Winter quietly disappears. She is busy when Kim calls; she cannot take her here or there. So Kim turns to me again...and I, glad to be free, want no repeat of last fall's bondage. Instead we play a game of one-upmanship, at which Kim is far more skillful than I. You do me a favor; I will do one for you. Kim offers to watch my children while I do errands. In return she will bring her laundry to my house, to do it while I am gone. Fair enough, but the chain of favors never ends. I come home in time to be in the house when Lisa gets home from school, only to find that Kim is not done with me.

"What you do now?" she asks.

"Nothing until Lisa gets here."

"Minh, she at dentist today. I watch Lisa, you pick up Minh?"

But I like to be home when Lisa walks in. I have been busy all afternoon; I want to sit for a while. Besides, Minh has taken the bus to the dentist and would probably be just as content to take it home. Unlike Kim, the girls are not intimidated by public transportation. No matter, Kim cannot stand to watch my car sit idle. I go. I enjoy talking to Minh, after all, and see her too little. As usual, Minh shares tidbits of gossip about the family Kim would be reluctant to tell, for fear of angering me. She even confides a secret about her name. "Minh," she says, "Usually name for a boy. My parents...I don't know. I think maybe they want a boy." She laughs. Of the children from her father's first wife, she is the youngest. There was only one boy. But among the second wife's five children were three boys, so Minh's services in the house as a daughter were welcome. The errands become a mixed blessing: the stories about the family are always welcome. It is easier to talk about ending the favors than to do it. If I bring Kim over to do laundry, score one for me, but then if she babysits I owe her something in return, the trip to the dentist's office...and on and on and on.

And soon she learns to trap me with the preliminaries, so that I give myself away and cannot say no. We seem to reach new heights of subtlety and good manners. One morning the phone rings early. I do not expect it to be Kim: I think maybe she is ill.

"How are you?" she asks, as if she has all the time in the world.

"Fine. And you?"

"Fine. How are your children?"

"Fine." Ah, already I should suspect. How does she expect my children to be?

"You take Mike to school today?"

"Yes." Of course I do. I have been taking him for months. She knows this perfectly well.

"You know, Lan...she not go to school today."

"Oh? Is she sick?" Perhaps that is it. Lan needs to see the doctor. It would be impolite to ask without inquiring about my own children first.

"No, she no sick. She miss bus."

At last I understand. So simple. A minor task: I inhale relief. "Oh. You want me to drive her to school after I drop Mike at the nursery school?"

"Oh...yes!" The tone of delight. She has made herself clear; she has won.

But oh for some good American directness. Of course I will be in Kim's neighborhood when I take Mike to school; of course I can drop by and get Lan. If only we could do without the first ten minutes of chit-chat, perhaps I would not feel so trapped. I resent the preliminaries that carefully rule out all alternatives. After Kim knows exactly what my schedule is, how can I possibly say no?

The game wears me down. I am always the loser. I am, after all, the one with the car. I become stern again and do less. Kim searches for a new benefactor, and this time I sense in her manner a tone of desperation. So many of the Americans are growing tired. Even the English tutors have not the indignation they had before. At last she finds a woman from Jonesville to help her. But Jonesville is ten miles away, too far for casual trips here and there, good only for the once-a-week visit to the doctor, and perhaps a stop in the supermarket on the way home. The Americans are running away...and no wonder. What thread has there been on which to string these friendships? Only Kim's needs and, in return for favors her unfailing courtesy, her easy cheer. How do you weigh work against good manners? In the end, the work grows heavier. Not much basis for enduring good will.

Now Minh, too, has been brought into the fray. Minh is doing housework once a week for Mrs. Sievers, the widow with the farm Ha and Tu used to live on. With all I have heard about Mrs. Sievers' demands, I am surprised. But Minh shakes her head. "She yell all the time," she admits, "but I like to help her because she sick." And this sounds like Minh to me, very Vietnamese. Fon's irresponsibility, Lan's laziness around the house, Mrs. Sievers' meanness...all are acceptable. People are what they are.

But no, there is an ulterior motive after all. Kim tells me that Mrs. Sievers has found her a doctor in Jonesburg, a general practitioner, who will treat her baby for free after it is born and who will treat the rest of the family too. Minh doesn't get paid much for the housework. The real reward is to be in medical care. To be on good terms with Americans still pays.

And yet in Minh and Lan there is a sort of pride developing too. One night, unable to find a babysitter in the neighborhood so we can go out, we ask them formally if they will come over to watch the children. When we return and try to pay them, they refuse to take our money. "We *like* to play with your children," they say. It seems it has never occurred to them that this is not simply expected of them. We tell them we always pay our sitters, that we will be hurt if they do not take the money. But they are adamant. We say they should think of sitting as a job, something they might consider doing during the summer. They laugh, as if the idea delights them as much as it surprises. "If we sit for you in the summer," they say, "then we don't mind taking money. But not now."

May...and Kim and I speak very little now that the issue of favors is a strain between us again. Minh and Lan tell us what little we hear. Fon has left Baltimore to live in a dormitory in Annapolis, with other refugees. All of them are working on the food service crew at the Naval Academy. He is not happy there—still he has not been able to work with his mind—but he no longer dreams of Florida or California. Soon he will move to Delaware, to live with a friend. "He no visit anymore," Lan says. "But he call."

Even during our rare phone conversations, Kim and I misunderstand each other. One day I end a call saying that we will have to get together soon—a typical American vagueness, and as it turns out, a cruel one. Kim, misinterpreting, thinks I mean to visit her apartment that very day. She cleans up hastily, and waits for me all afternoon. When I do not appear, she is hurt but afraid to call me back. We hear of the incident only when Quang mentions it casually to Ben, an item of gossip, as if it were of no importance. Both of us, I think, regret the trust we have lost.

On May 28, Quang goes to work and Kim goes into labor. Rather than call him home (would it be unseemly to disturb him on the job? do they feel they owe even this important time to Ben?), Kim phones her friend from Jonesburg, who takes her to the doctor's office. After all, the baby is not due until June. The doctor says she is in early labor and sends her home. From what I can gather, she spends most of the day there alone. The friend returns to Jonesburg. She does not call me, and whether she consults Yen or Ha I do not know. Van, her other friend, is surely at work. I will always wonder whether Kim felt it would be wrong to call me—I have made so much of her being independent—or whether she is just too far removed now to want me there. Whatever the reason, I am hurt and feel guilty that I have let things go this far. I would have liked to have been in on this new beginning. When Quang returns from work at five, he takes Kim to the hospital. She has her baby, a boy, Tom, at eight. Minh calls us shortly after to give us the news.

The next day we visit her in the hospital. Already she looks better than she has in months, as if she has managed to shed the dark cast of her pregnancy with the afterbirth. The baby, in his little crib in the nursery, looks exactly like Quang.

Tom, Kim tells us, is an Americanization of a Vietnamese name, Tuan. Spelled our way, it is a little of both. We rise to go, having heard the story of the birth, having presented baby clothes and flowers. Kim looks up at us and smiles, as if she has remembered something important.

"You know," she tells us beaming, "Tommy is an American."

PART TWO

RESOLUTION AND CHANGE

ELEVEN

During the summer of 1976, except through the normal routine of work, we saw Kim and Quang very little. Though we were away part of the time and the children busy with their activities, the real reason for our breach was that we were all exhausted. Tommy was born; the great strain of Kim's pregnancy was over. The tug-of-war for goods and favors had gone on for so long and become so aggravating for both sides that neither could continue to hold on. We had either to call a halt or end—as the church sponsorships had—in permanent enmity. With Quang still working for Ben and his family living in town, the temporary cease-fire made more sense. So it was not until the end of the summer that we began to resume our accustomed social relationship...and found, to our surprise, that something astonishing had happened. Gone was the listless Kim of the winter and spring, reluctant to do for herself and yearning to be cared for like a child. Unlike most women who are stunned by the responsibility of a first infant, Kim recovered at once. Off she would go to Washington for the day with Vietnamese friends, Tommy in tow—a feat few women would attempt with a six-week-old baby. Her resilience was back and she seemed anxious to get on with the life that, during the pregnancy, had been held in abeyance. Was this the Kim who six months before refused to go half a mile on a public bus? Even Quang, who had resisted learning to drive with every excuse imaginable (cheap cars were too old, the repair bills too high, the insurance too expensive) was being given lessons by his friends. After a year of pallor and weakness, sudden healing. The family showed signs of a returning strength.

And why the sudden burst of confidence? Many things, all inter-woven, not the least of which was that the American benefactors had disappeared, and the refugees—forced to rely on each other for support—found they could manage very well. Their English, an insurmountable problem six months before, was now fluent enough that they could deal with strangers. Most of them were financially independent, though not yet affluent. Many of the confusions of earlier months now cleared up through simple improved understanding. The result was a feeling of freedom and acceptance that was the first happy surprise most of them had had in a year.

The language in particular came as a surprise to us as well. We had been quick to credit Minh and Lan with fluency: girls in school are supposed to learn rapidly. But we still thought of Kim and Quang as non-English-speaking, able to communicate with Ben and me and the few sympathetic friends through a jumble of words and gestures. It was not until the phone rang one day while I was at Kim's apartment on a brief errand that I realized she, too, had gradually acquired the skills to cope with the world at large. Instead of issuing forth in the expected burst of Vietnamese, Kim conducted the conversation smoothly in English. The caller, a stranger, had reached the wrong number. Kim explained that she had missed by a single digit, suggested she try again, and exchanged the appropriate niceties. No longer did she hide behind her accent, pretending not to understand. Where from our standpoint Kim and Quang had seemed to avoid confrontation outside of their closed circle whenever they could, from their own perspective it must have become apparent, finally, that confrontation was inevitable...and now, no longer afraid, they were ready to meet it head on.

Their improving financial status, such as it was, must have been heady, too. After a fall and winter in which the battle over welfare programs had been made more bitter by bureaucratic rules they didn't understand, which seemed unfairly to exclude them, now government aid unfolded in all its tawdriness, as their friends and acquaintances gradually participated in every program available. Ha and Tu's townhouse in the projects was oven-hot all summer while their own apartment with its high ceilings stayed relatively cool. Unlike Ha's baby, Tommy did not suffer unduly from the heat. And in July, when Ha went to work in the sewing factory where their other good friend, Van, had started months earlier, the increased family income made Tu's family ineligible for most of the welfare they had been receiving. Their rent subsidy was cut, with the result that Tu paid about the same for the shabby townhouse in the projects as Kim and Quang did for their own, nicer apartment. Ha's children were no longer eligible for either food stamps or Medicaid. Tu covered them under his own hospitalization plan at work—at considerable extra expense. Whether what we had said about cut-off points and self-support had been misunderstood before, or whether we were simply not believed, now it seemed to make no difference. Seeing firsthand that the welfare programs indeed had their conditions—and that they applied to everyone equally—Kim and Quang began to accept their ineligibility rather than fight against it. Besides, contrary to what they had once believed, welfare did not provide the lifestyle they had in mind. They quietly withdrew their application for public housing. The undercurrent of conniving and distrust vanished. Reality had dawned, and been accepted, and they began to plan their lives along a course which did not rely for its mainstay on begging.

This was especially encouraging at a time when virtually all the American benefactors had disappeared. The English tutors now did no more than teach. Mrs. Carson, the school's director, had newer, needier immigrants to consume her attention. Even the woman from Jonesburg dropped out of the picture shortly after Tommy's birth. So for the genuine emotional support they needed, that everyone needs, Kim and Quang turned to the other refugees remaining in Crestville, and they to them.

The time seemed ripe for it. By late spring the exodus to the big cities had slowed, and the remaining refugee families in town were planning to stay. There were not many of them—Ha and Tu, Van and Trinh, two other families with older children, and Yen and her American husband—but enough that they were able to form a close circle. After a year of upheaval, when nothing must have looked permanent or reliable, suddenly there was a kind of solidity. They drove each other to Holiday Park, to the Chinese grocery, they went to Washington and Baltimore on weekends, to visit friends and buy staples at the Vietnamese stores which are beginning to appear, they taught Quang to drive. And from their mood, this mutual helping was perhaps the best thing that had happened to them so far. For this very solidity their refugee neighbors had fled to the cities, to peers who could offer the reliability the Americans would not. And now, though it had taken longer, they had that solidity in Crestville. Whatever misunderstandings remained with the Americans, they mattered less because there were other Vietnamese to rely on—and this gave them strength.

Time and a little perspective have given us some new thoughts. Why have the refugees been shotgunned throughout the country this way? No group before them has ever been told, even initially, *where* to settle. Even the Cubans, airlifted to Miami in '59 and the early 60's, were set down among their own, among friends. What would my grandparents have done without their uncles and cousins who spoke Yiddish that first year or two? There was no welfare in those days, and no American sympathizers either, but as we look out from the confusion of this past year, the image of those poverty-stricken Russian Jews holding each other up looks like luxury, emotionally at least, compared to what the Vietnamese have had. Was the spreading out necessary because the refugees came all at once and in such great numbers? Was the idea to assimilate them quickly or just to make sure they weren't too apparent in any one place, to remind us we had not won the war in Southeast Asia? Unlike my European grandparents, Vietnamese faces are that much easier to spot in the landscape. But pepper them lightly throughout the country and maybe no one will notice; there will be no great welfare burden on any one state. All very nice in theory, but a little crueler if you happen to be one of the refugees caught in the crunch. What must it be like to be penniless, in a cold climate for the first time—not by choice—and under the thumb of Americans whose idea of help seems less benevolent than simply indecipherable, because the only vocabulary you share is maybe fifty words of niceties? Recipe for a frustrating year. Perhaps the astonishing thing is that Kim and Quang seemed to be recovering so quickly.

And one more question: why were we not warned? Looking back over this journal, I see a litany of anger, frustration and guilt. If Kim and Quang have been keeping their own records, they cannot make happier reading. Was there no one, going in, who had any idea what problems we were likely to encounter, we the Americans, or "we" the refugees? In all this long year we have received not one piece of written information from anyone—Catholic Charities (except for their monthly how-to-get-it newsletter), the federal government, anyone—offering guidelines on what to expect. Can it be that no one knew? There were not many settled Vietnamese in this country before the refugees arrived, but surely there were *some*. Surely they had their own difficulties adjusting and could have offered us all some advice, if not in government pamphlets then in the newspapers, on TV. I haven't seen it. Why?

Ben says it's because everyone wants to forget. In his hometown in Indiana, a family planned to sponsor a refugee family and was met with such strong opposition from the community that finally the application was withdrawn, for fear the refugees would come to physical harm. Here in Crestville, there has been no such public outcry. The churches are warmly, if not always practically, sympathetic, and everyone else mumbles quietly, if at all. The stonemasons still dislike working with a *gook*; the *gook's* job could be filled by an American (Could it? Ben looks long and hard for laborers, and finds few who would rather work than draw unemployment, which brings nearly as much). The Stevens' complain, grumble, and finally alienate. We do not like to be reminded that we abandoned the Vietnamese to their fate, Ben says, and have some responsiblity for those who escaped it by coming here. The great national silence takes precedence over the personal suffering of a hundred thousand refugees and the people who bumblingly tried to help them, so that the rest of us can feel comfortable in our easy chairs.

For myself, the silence was annoying because it reinforced our personal guilt. While all the difficulties were going on last fall and winter, while we were being criticized by the language school people who were only marginally involved themselves, the same conflicts were arising between refugees and sponsors all around us...if only we had known. The refugees talked to each other openly, but the sponsors did not. We each assumed our problems were unique, that there was some flaw in our particular method of handling the situation which was causing the difficulties, and this made us the more silent, because the more ashamed. Not until spring, when some of the refugees left, did the first stories of defeat and bitterness trickle out to alert us that we were not alone. If we had known sooner and been able to talk to each other, how many of the problems might have been resolved before they became unsolveable? Some, surely. A couple of newspaper stories about the conflicts and we might have felt less isolated. We might have been able to cope.

So at last we come to summer, to this great reversal of fortunes, to healing. Not everything has changed, but enough. Minh, looking for summer work, was still doing housecleaning once a week for Mrs. Sievers because Mrs. Sievers continued her interest, no longer with direct goods or favors, but with influence. After finding Kim a doctor who would treat Tommy for free, her campaign shifted to lobbying the hospital board to cancel Kim's maternity bill...at which she was eventually successful. We objected, thinking Kim and Quang should pay the bill even if it meant sending $5 a month for years, or dipping into the saved subsidy money. But though Kim and Quang were glad enough to take the hospital's charity, they now regarded it as something out of the ordinary, not what was to be expected in the regular run of things...and we took this as a good sign.

By August, with welfare a dead issue behind them, Kim and Quang decided it was time for Kim to go to work. She had been bottle-feeding Tommy from the beginning, just in case. Of all the Vietnamese women we've known who've had babies since their arrival, not one has breastfed, though generally this would have proved cheaper. The bottle seemed to have for the refugees the same appeal it did for American women in the 40's—the promise of freedom, a way to get out, a second income. And so at the end of August, leaving Tommy with Minh and Lan until school started, then with a day-care mother who watched Van's two preschoolers, Kim went to work in the sewing factory with Van and Ha. It was a special source of pride with her that other Vietnamese, not Americans, had gotten her the job.

"The Vietnamese women work very good," Kim told us. "They do more than the Americans. The man tell Van, 'Bring all you friends. We hire all you Vietnamese friends.'" Paid on a piecework basis, Van was already clearing nearly $5 an hour. Kim was confident of soon doing the same. The company had a union shop, so much per month for hospitalization and life insurance and a liberal leave policy, all the things Quang, working for Ben, lacked. What Kim did not realize at first was how much more difficult her life would be. Leaving the house at 5:30 in the morning so she could ride in a carpool, she would work four or six hours—whatever was available on a given day—and then wait in the lounge until the others got off, only to reach home at 4:30 to begin on the chores there—feeding Tommy his supper, helping with dinner for the rest of the family, cleaning up. By mid-September she looked tired and drawn; we expected the complaints to begin again. We dreaded a new yearning for welfare. It never came. Apparently she felt ready to earn her own way.

By the end of the summer we felt we had come nearly full circle in all respects but one: Quang's job. In the year that had just passed, Ben's company had grown from a five-man operation (two framing crews and a laborer) to nearly double that. Matthew, who had arrived in March, had worked his way through the building process and was ready to take over as project manager at the site. Ben was searching for an office in town to supplement the construction trailer. One of the new men had quickly worked his way from labor to framing, while Quang stayed behind, doing the same things he had done a year before.

As the summer progressed, Ben decided he had figured how Quang operated, if only he could put it to use. Unlike the American workers, Quang never went all-out for an hour or two, only to collapse into a 20-minute coffee break. Instead, he worked at about three-quarter efficiency all the time, pacing himself, compensating for his physical smallness so that he would never get too tired to go on, never speeding up or slowing down. At the end of the day, he had put out about the same amount of effort as the others, only in quite a different manner.

But knowing Quang's *modus operandi* did nothing to relieve the difficulties it created. If his work was actually on a par with everyone else's, still he managed to make it look as if it weren't—as if he were shuffling while the others were running, working carelessly, not interested in whether he accomplished anything or not. "Most guys psych themselves up for work," said the carpenter, Craig. "Quang psychs himself down." Ben felt that even if Quang were ready for promotion—which he wasn't—that moving him up would have a bad effect on morale.

And ultimately Quang's attitude began to have its adverse effect on other areas as well. When at last—after a summer of lessons—he was ready to go for his driver's test, he passed the written section with a perfect score. Then, as I looked on, he immediately failed the driving. Whether because he misunderstood or simply wasn't paying attention, he put the car in reverse instead of drive, backing it into the chain link fence behind it. The next week, when Ben took him for a second try, he failed again. This time he knocked down the posts that marked the parking spaces. Two tests, and he had yet to get on the street.

"And then," Ben said, "he had the nerve to get out of the car *smiling*. I told him it's one thing to fail, but you damn well better not be happy about it." Ben fumed over the incident for a week. It seemed to him indicative of Quang's whole problem—his passive willingness to accept criticism without becoming angry enough to change. But as if to give the lie to that, Quang had a Vietnamese friend take him for his third attempt at the driving test...and he passed. Ben began sending him on errands with the company truck, to build his confidence. For weeks Quang drove on the center line down the middle of the divided highway, steering frantically. If he survived, Ben said, it would have been good practice.

Then Stevens lowered the boom. On the first of September he announced he was not intending to renew Quang's lease. For all the troubles of the past year, the frictions and unexpected visitors and rent hikes, the family was nevertheless shocked and upset at the news. Suddenly the value of their apartment fully dawned on them. It was bigger and better located than what most of their friends had and no more expensive. Stevens was no longer even marginally cordial. Quang was now the little *gook*. When Ben advised Quang not to pay his last month's rent, but instead to live on the security deposit, Stevens called our house late one night, nasty-drunk, with curses and shouting. Ben, worried about the family's welfare that last month, told Stevens we could probably sue him for discrimination if we wanted to—a threat which subsequently kept him quiet. And yet for all the unpleasantness, which put us into sympathy with Quang, we felt that again it was Quang's attitude that was partly to blame. The trash, coming down the chute loose, had always been a problem...but how well had he handled it? How neatly cleaned up? How many empty bottles and shreds of newspaper left lying behind on the basement floor? And what did Stevens see when he visited the building to check? A tenant doing his best...or only the inattention to detail, the shuffling gait, the inability to hustle? The slanted eyes.

The final month of Quang's lease flew past. He made a few half-hearted attempts to find housing, nothing serious. The family seemed to feel that if they ignored the problem, it would go away. Or maybe, for all their new confidence, such a large undertaking as moving was simply beyond them.

"Did you look at the ads in the paper?" we asked, laying out the classified.

"Sometime," Quang would say.

The month ended, the lease expired. None of the Vietnamese families, their good friends, offered to take them in. Reluctantly, we moved Steve back into our bedroom, Mike in with Lisa, and re-arranged the two front bedrooms for the family again. More than a year had passed, full circle...and we were back to "GO."

TWELVE

I was wrong: having Kim's family move back in with us again was in no way a return to the parent-child relationship of the year before. On the contrary, it was pleasant for all of us, and restored the closeness we had lost over the winter. Kim and Quang were at work all day while Tommy stayed with a day-care mother; the girls were at school. We shared only our dinners, and with them fragments of our now quite separate lives. And together we looked for an apartment.

Experience had taught us to run a House—Wanted ad in the classified, not wait to see what the rental columns would bring. In addition, a new government housing project was just opening near downtown. We sent Quang to investigate. He returned with the news—no surprise—that since he would be ineligible for subsidy, he would have to pay quite a high rent. For the price, he was not interested, and we were just as glad, having avoided government housing this long.

Eventually our ad brought us a phone call from the owner of half a double townhouse just across the street from Van and Trinh. The landlord turned out to be a small, soft-spoken man, almost the exact opposite of the burly Stevens. "I lived here myself for fifteen years," he told us. "I'm looking for a family who'll take care of it." It seemed not to occur to him that he was being especially benevolent renting to Vietnamese—a great plus, we thought.

The place is smaller than the Stevens apartment but with both upstairs and downstairs as well as a nice back yard, and the rent is about the same except that now Quang will have to pay the oil bill. No more free utilities. They moved after staying with us only two weeks, and again we went our more or less separate ways. One afternoon about a month later Kim called to ask us if we would watch Tommy while the family went to a wedding. It was the first time she had left him here, a measure of our new trust.

And so began the story of the house, of the family's new affluence, for Kim's incoming salary soon began to be felt. One thing she had always hated was the old gas stove at Stevens' apartment, which leaked and smelled. Now there was a hookup for an electric stove ...and Kim immediately found a used one, a smoothtop like ours, through an ad in the paper.

"The lady say $200," she told me. "I say too much. She say $150. I say $75. I buy for $100." Considering that the stove looked brand new and worked fine and that in the store it would have cost about $500, it was an excellent buy. But I worried. Since the beginning, Kim had judged the value of goods by what we had in our house...the potato peeler with the decorative handle, the color TV, the smoothtop stove. It seemed not to occur to her that we were older than she was by more than a decade and had acquired things as our finances improved and our family grew. Were we now to play a game of who-has-the-better? I had always thought of myself as basically disinterested in *things*. Certain Kim must not have thought so, to want to involve me in this contest. (Or maybe her behavior only mirrors mine and that's what makes me squirm, showing me what a materialist I really am.) Eventually we came to the same impasse we reached a year ago when she was picking through the Rescue Mission's furniture. So she wanted a smoothtop stove. Who was I to object? She had paid for it herself; she was a breadwinner now. And what's more, she had leafed through the ads herself, made a trip to a strange house, bargained in English, things we had once spent months urging her to try. My concern quickly faded.

But the stove was not to be the end of it. In the middle of November a huge console color TV appeared in the living room, startling next to the Rescue Mission's used furniture, with a wide screen, remote control, ornately carved cabinet. The set had cost a thousand dollars easily, and had been financed through the store, which had called to confirm Quang's employment. I was skeptical.

"Well, why not?" said Ben, reacting to my suggestion that we advise sticking to used—or at least modest—merchandise first, then working up. "How much do you think they spend on entertainment otherwise?" And the set, of which they were very proud, seemed more than an introduction to easy credit. It was a symbol of independence, of their ability to do for themselves. All last year we had told them a color TV was something to save for, not ask for, something to buy. And now they had.

The TV was followed shortly after New Year's by a car. More than the two previous purchases, for which we could understand both the practical and psychological need, the car gave us concern. "Why not a used car?" Ben had asked months before. Quang rejected the idea vehemently. "My friend, his car no work," he said. "It take three weeks to fix it. Then he pay two hundred dollar." None of his friends speak unaccented English, he explained. The mechanics view them as sitting ducks. They overcharge, they do incomplete work. The cars must be taken back repeatedly, and service is slow. A horror story. Quang would rather pay a larger monthly payment than put up with repairs.

Even in view of that, the car he bought was exceptional, a new blue Mustang with every optional extra: tinted glass, bucket seats, white wall tires, air conditioning. Significantly, Matthew had bought a car several months before, a Pinto, also blue, but not so fancy. We couldn't help feeling Quang was trying to show he was on an equal— or better—footing with us materially. As if we had pushed him so far on the issue of self-support that now he had to flaunt it.

The car caused quite a stir at work. There was something unsettling to the men about the lowest laborer arriving on the job in such luxury. They all seemed to feel that the first car anyone buys shouldn't be quite so perfect. Most of the others drive old clunkers; even Matthew's Pinto was a poor second best to Quang's. And Ben's work car is an old Chevelle he's been driving for years, with the back seat removed to make room for tools. The American mind-set again: you work *up* to the best.

I'm not immune to these uncharitable musings myself. My own first car was a $50 junker which I was delighted to have. When I met Ben years later, he convinced me I could afford a new car on my instructor's salary. Climbing out of the dead-battery-on-a-cold morning class was one of life's great pleasures. Having suffered, I suppose I expect Quang to suffer too. So the men at work looked askance at Quang's car, and try as I might I couldn't help thinking that the color TV as well might more prudently have been a portable, not the top of the line. It was as if the family were saying to us, "Look, we came to this country to have these things, and if you won't give them to us, see how quickly we can get them ourselves."

Only Ben regarded the new acquisitions as a sign of health. To him the TV and the car were the first signs of aggressiveness he'd seen in Quang, however subtle. If only the feelings could be transferred into positive action on the job. He was disturbed only by what seemed too massive an outlay of money. Last year, it looked as if the family would be swallowed by the welfare system. This year, it was more likely to be the Great American Credit Plan.

In January 1977, Kim invited us over for an elaborate dinner celebrating Tet...and we saw that, much as we had reservations about their new buying habits, their recent financial independence had such an effect on their confidence that the tensions that had once existed between us had all but disappeared. Over heaping plates of pork and carrots mixed with rice, shrimp chips fried in oil, and Kim's pork-filled eggrolls, we shared our first joke about ourselves.

"In Vietnam, one person eats maybe four cups of rice at dinner," Lan said.

"Four cups? Not that much!" I insisted. But Lan maintained it was so. Suddenly we were able to picture ourselves when the family first came to stay with us, when I would put maybe three cups of rice on the table for both families. We all laughed, remembering that each of us wondered constantly what the other was thinking, remembering how hard we all tried to be polite. It had taken us a year and a half to see the humour in our situation.

Also that night we learned that, despite the family's apparent confidence, there was still one thing about which they continued to feel insecure. After a year of displacement—from Vietnam to the Philippines to Guam to Indiantown Gap to our house to their own apartment—they had finally begun to feel settled when Stevens evicted them, and they were still badly shaken. After our hasty search, the townhouse was proving both less comfortable and more expensive than the apartment had been. Even as we sat there, the furnace turned on and off incessantly, heating the small rooms quickly, then allowing the air to cool down while everyone felt chilled. A sign of an oversized furnace, Ben said and Quang confirmed this, showing him a recent oil bill which had turned out to be higher than he'd expected

Kim and Quang revealed to us their new fear: of being forever trapped between unsympathetic landlords and unsuitable accommodations. The apartment had met their needs, but there they had had to contend with Stevens' fiery prejudice. Now the landlord was more humane, but the townhouse itself left so much to be desired. Able to afford some of the American comforts they'd yearned for, they were discovering that the most important one of all—security in their home—eluded them. They had had enough of being displaced. "But I no see what we can do," Kim said.

To this Ben has his own answer. Save for a house. "In a year or two you ought to begin thinking about buying," he said. "You don't have to rent forever. You can look for an inexpensive house first, and then fix it up—Quang knows how to do that now—and sell it at a higher price so you can move someplace better." It was as if we had introduced them to a fascinating new game. So they could *buy*. It was not necessary to live under the thumb of landlords forever. Even prejudice could be mitigated by the dollar. They looked at each other in wonder, as if Ben had shown them the end of a dark tunnel.

What surprised us was that the family waited not a few years but less than two months before asking Ben to tell them specifically how to go about looking for a house. In late February, with the car purchase behind them, Quang told Ben that Kim had been given more hours to work, nearly a full day, and was making almost as much as he was. With $2,000 saved for a down payment, they felt they could now afford *something*, and wanted Ben to tell them what.

I was doubly astonished: first that they had any money at all left after the TV and the car, and secondly that Kim was moving up so quickly at work while Quang continued his accustomed slow and steady and infuriatingly even pace. The mystery of the money gave way to some quick calculations...and again I found myself irritated, if only by my ingrained American values.

If Kim and Quang had $2,000, we figured it must have come from the original government subsidy money, plus interest earned on it, plus whatever the family had been able to save over the past year. The down payments for the car and TV must have come from Kim's earnings, while they lived on Quang's. I found myself wondering what—if they *had* been eligible for welfare last year—they would have done with Quang's salary, which they then claimed was inadequate. Now it seemed to support them quite decently, if most of Kim's earnings could go for luxuries. Like Nga and O, the people who had asked neighbors to get them furniture before they moved to Baltimore, though they had $1,000 saved, Kim and Quang must have been determined not to dip into their savings no matter what. But to me it was unthinkable that they preferred to tell their English teachers they were going hungry than to admit the savings existed.

Ben warned me not to be too critical. "We don't know. We've never had absolutely nothing. If we did, we'd want to hang onto that government money too." Possibly so, and then tight-fistedness was a good strategy. But I couldn't shake the notion that it was dishonest to ask for more when there were savings in the bank. I would have felt better if they'd paid the hospital and the obstetrician some token amount...or if they were paying Tommy's doctor now rather than laying out their savings for a thousand-dollar TV. As much as I struggled, my Puritan ethics dogged me. Easy to pass judgment, of course, since I was moralizing at their expense.

Whatever I thought, everyone now turned to the task of finding Kim and Quang a house under $30,000, under $20,000 if possible. In that price range Quang would be looking for a handyman's special, something with cosmetic defects but no structural ones, not an easy item to find. Ben told them to begin checking the ads and visiting open houses, to get an idea what fair market values were. He agreed to look at anything Quang thought promising. Considering the condition of many older houses in the area, we thought he was in for a long search.

By April the house had become a real obsession with the family. Quang brought a realtor over here one night, so that Ben could help explain to him what the family wanted. When eventually the realtor showed them some properties and Kim said they were all too expensive, Ben advised them to begin looking primarily at sale-by-owner homes. With a realtor trying to ask top dollar, with his 6% commission tacked onto whatever the owner expected to get, many of the lower-range properties were priced right out of Quang's market. Once they learned to look, they kept themselves very busy, spending all their weekends at it, and some evenings.

In mid-April Quang found what he thought might be his first real possibility. Half a double only a few blocks away from his townhouse, it was priced at $14,000, which sounded to Quang like a real bargain. When Ben looked, however, he discovered a roof that needed replacing immediately and a furnace that was about to wear out. He advised against it, saying that nevertheless he was impressed by what Quang was doing.

"He's looking at the areas between downtown and the new suburbs, where the houses will hold their value but where the prices aren't particularly inflated," he told me. "A house that needs work, but in a solid neighborhood."

I was still unable to share his enthusiasm. Between the car and the TV and now the mad rush for a house it seemed to me that now the family was all too anxious to part with their money. Ben suggested another answer. "If you come from a country like Vietnam, where inflation is so high and money is so unstable, perhaps the *last* thing you want is a savings account," he said. Even if they could believe that money here was really safer, there was logic behind their actions. "The things they're buying aren't frivolous," he insisted; they were not expensive clothes or the trinkets Kim liked to look at in the shops, but only what they had planned for. After two years of rigid budgeting, they could not help being impatient.

"Quang is just becoming a capitalist," Ben said.

And so, capitalist that he was, Quang found his house at the beginning of May. Located only two blocks from the city park, on a street lined with big old trees, it was half a double in the sort of neighborhood that never deteriorates no matter how old the houses get. The streets are narrow and winding, punctuated by little circles which are planted out in canna bulbs in summer. The house itself was brick and frame with a big front porch. It had a charm the rented townhouse certainly lacked. For months while we awaited settlement, I heard about the interior which I had yet to see: four bedrooms, two baths, living room, dining room and kitchen. The upstairs had been used as an apartment for some years, so there would be work to do to convert the rooms back into bedrooms. No matter, Kim and Quang were ready. They were more elated than we had ever seen them.

Settlement hinged on the bank's approving Quang's financing, which took its characteristic sweet time. Ben had referred Quang to the savings and loan that handled his own houses, so the delay was caused only by the slow moving of the creaky bureaucratic process— which in itself was enough to create a certain amount of tension. The lady who owned the house was quite old, ready to move into a nursing home. Her daughter called us regularly, trying to speed things up. She was worried that her mother would die before the closing and that the monies from the house would go into her estate rather than directly to her, the daughter, as apparently was the plan. The result of all this haste was that Kim and Quang were able to buy the house for only $16,000. After the $2,000 down payment and with a long-term mortgage, their monthly payments would be well within range. The settlement date was set up at last, for the end of the summer.

On May 28, as a last fling in the townhouse, Kim had a huge party to celebrate Tommy's first birthday. First birthdays are very important in Vietnam, she explained to us: after that, birthdays are generally ignored. For the occasion, there was to be a lavish cookout in the back yard, with Minh in charge of barbequing chicken. Not only did all the families from Crestville turn out, but large numbers of friends from Baltimore as well, mostly young men who spent their time with Minh, Lan and Lan's friend, Nguyen. Not until then did we realize how much the girls had matured. Lan, always beautiful, pretended haughty disinterest in her group of admirers. And now Minh had come to look like a young woman too. She had let her hair grow all winter—no more girlish Dutch-boy—so that now it hung thick and dark below her shoulders as she presided over the chicken and talked to her friends.

In other ways, too, the girls had changed. Lan, suddenly practical, was intent on revising her school curriculum to include more business courses. We consented, flattered that she still looked to us for advice, but encouraged her to take all the requirements for college too, since her Vietnamese schools had been so far ahead of ours in math that she would be in a good position to get a scholarship. We worried too that the push for money *now*, for things *now* was infectious. Ben gave his standard speech on the value of college, just to be sure Lan's long-term thinking hadn't become clouded only to discover that her real concern was with summer jobs, which are tight. She thought a little bookkeeping, a smattering of typing, might help.

"We will babysit if we have to," Minh told us, "but we don't like to babysit." Groans from us. How different from their attitude when they first came here, when they took over the children without even being asked. Maybe we had been too pleased to see them become so Americanized. Their happy attitude about children was one of the nicest things they brought. Who knows what else will go before they're completely comfortable here?

A Vietnamese party, un-American in its niceness. Such generosity for a one-year-old child. Yen made Tommy a gorgeous four-tiered birthday cake, more like a wedding cake except that the decorations were in bright reds and greens and blues, no wan pastels like those on our American bakery cakes. The leftover batter went into cupcakes, also with the bright decorations. Mike and Lisa, unused to such things, were delighted. With their Vietnamese friends who now speak fluent English, they squealed over the cakes and stuffed themselves with icing, unaware of the frictions that still haunt their elders. How many Americans would make such a cake for the little boy of a friend? And as for Yen, what was her reward that first year, when she took the part of her refugee friends? However misguided we still think she was, it could not have been easy. When it comes to enduring personal discomfort for each other, the Vietnamese are more charitable than we are, no question. And at the party Yen was all smiles, as if no harsh word had ever passed between us, as if she, like Kim and Quang, is incapable of holding a grudge.

More shows of generosity: the presents. Tommy, of all the children, seemed to enjoy them the least. He cried through the cutting of the cake and most of the opening of packages, though finally he calmed down when it dawned on him what was in the boxes. Such gifts! Complete outfits, riding toys, tables and chairs, none of your little pail-and-shovel dime-store stuff, even from the young people who cannot have much money. Perhaps this is what makes us uncomfortable: seeing the Vietnamese so giving with each other, so generous, yet finding when they demand the same from us that we resist—it is not in our culture to be that way. For us it is important to do for ourselves...and still at the same time we feel ashamed.

The chicken gone, the cake eaten, the adults sit on lawn chairs reminiscing about life as it was for them two years ago when they first arrived. An American neighbor has eaten and left: Ben and I are the only non-Vietnamese in the group. Everyone speaks English for our benefit, and is very nice, even confidential, as if we have passed some sort of test and now at last are to be trusted. So many times I thought our relationship with Kim and Quang would end disastrously; so many times Ben insisted it wouldn't if we remained open, available even when we disagreed. It turns out he is going to be right. Most of the refugees are now content, they say. They laugh about their early experiences. Only Ha is still openly bitter. Her life here has not proved sweet.

"When I work for Mrs. Sievers," she tells us, "I cry every day. She never see me cry, but I do. I never do housework before, and she always yell at me: 'Do this! Do that, be careful!' Now I still work hard but I am independent. I don't like to belong to somebody."

But independence is not enough; life is too hard. Ha works day and night and longs for her country. Even her children do not understand, and this makes her more bitter yet. Her children speak only in English; she is afraid they will forget their Vietnamese. "My children, they like it here," she says sourly. "But I will...*never*."

Going home, Ben remarks on the irony of Ha being the malcontent. Ha, who had so much given to her at the start—a free house and food stamps and Medicaid—Ha is the most disappointed. Perhaps it is because she was a teacher at home, with servants to care for her house and children. She knows now she cannot expect that here. Or perhaps it is because no one ever made clear when those initial handouts would stop. I think about Yen's cake and the elaborate presents. Perhaps the misunderstandings were inevitable. Such a wide gap between our own version of generosity and the Vietnamese one—how else should they have met but with misunderstanding? How tight-fisted we must have seemed when Kim wanted only a picture frame, only a long red dress, only a job. Had our roles been reversed, wouldn't she have provided them for *me*? And now, two years later, does she understand we were doing it on principle, now that Ha is still living in a cramped public project and Kim is about to move into a house of her own?

THIRTEEN

In September 1977, just a little over two years after their arrival in Crestville, Kim and Quang moved into their house. For all its exterior charm, the house inside was a study in decay. The woman who had owned it, ill herself, had provided no real upkeep for years. Plaster fell from the walls and ceilings in nearly every room; the bathrooms were a maze of rusted fixtures and rotting linoleum. The kitchen, small and bare except for a chipping porcelain sink in one corner, needed complete redoing. No matter, it was a house and it was theirs. A little imagination, a little elbow-grease and the possibilities were endless. Adjacent to the kitchen and separated from it by a wall was a large dining area, with huge old built-in cabinets on one end, eight feet high, and across from them a window overlooking the yard, potentially very pleasant. The family room, once a formal dining room, was dominated by a large bay window jutting out the side, creating a feeling of air and light. It was a house that could become whatever they would make of it.

A long hard winter followed, during which we saw Kim and Quang very little. The news was that they were busy remodelling. Even before the weather turned cold, Quang repainted the big front porch. The experience did what two years on the job hadn't: it taught him to be careful. After the porch, there were no more two-toned down-spouts, no more unstained trim strips at work.

"Being a homeowner forces you to worry about details whether you want to or not," Ben said. "Quang's still sloppier than I like, but the major mess-ups...I think he may be beyond them." Even Matthew, always more interested in Quang's performance than his cultural background, noticed the difference. Ben felt that he'd won a victory.

At Easter Kim invited us for dinner, to show us what they'd done. The difference was astounding. The two of them must have spent every weekend and many evenings at work. Quang had panelled the living room and drywalled the worst of the walls in the rest of the house, then repainted. Kim had papered the eating area in a cheerful print; Quang had put down new vinyl flooring. They had added counter space along the bare walls in the kitchen. In the living and family rooms Quang had taken strips of leftover carpet from work and created a pattern, very professional-looking, until the floors were covered wall to wall. He had begun to move the carpet up the stairs toward the bedrooms. For someone who paid no attention to detail, the work was awfully good.

I'd half expected to walk into the house and find it fully furnished too, now that Kim had discovered the installment plan. On the contrary, the Rescue Mision's bedroom furniture was still in evidence upstairs; and downstairs, where Kim had discarded the worst pieces, the rooms were generally bare. Her one major purchase had been a breakfast set: practical formica table but lavish, Spanish-style chairs, high in the back, trimmed in wrought iron, with deeply padded seats...in red, of course. I could picture Kim scouting the stores for just such a set, imagine her delight when she found it. As it turned out, that was not how it had happened. The breakfast set was bought used, and almost by accident.

"We go to buy...what?" Kim told me, puzzled. "You cut grass with it."

"A lawn mower?"

"Yes. The man want $50 for the lawn mower and $100 for the table and chairs. I say too much. We buy all together for $75."

"Quite a bargain," I said. Obviously I had been naive. With that kind of shrewdness, Kim was unlikely to be snared by material purchases. The American credit system was not going to do her in after all.

As always, there was one sour note. Kim has been allergic to the local trees and pollens ever since she came here. At the Stevens' apartment it wasn't much of a problem, since she was surrounded by concrete. At the townhouse she spent her summers with a stopped-up head. Now, living among big old trees and lush vegetation, her allergies started acting up as soon as the grass turned green.

Summer came and with it what must have been a time of confusion for Quang. The excitement over his new attention to not spilling paint and stain had worn off. Quang's infuriatingly slow pace did not pick up. Matthew became more and more impatient with him. Ben insisted that Quang did as much work as anyone, only in a different way. Matthew argued that even if that were so, it still looked as if they were tolerating laziness and was a bad influence on the other men. Nearly three years had passed and Quang was still only a mediocre laborer. They had tried repeatedly to work him onto a framing crew, without success. Now, as a compromise, they decided to let him be their runner, to pick up supplies like nails they needed periodically at the site.

Initially, Ben was optimistic. "He's the only one we can count on to come right back without stopping at the 7-11 for half an hour on the way," he said. This might be the perfect job for Quang, where his slow-and-steady pace would help him. That was in early May. By the end of the month it had become clear that the lumber company salesmen misunderstood his speech as often as not. Unlike Kim and the girls, Quang dropped nearly half of his consonants. Ben and Matthew were used to that, but even I, who saw him often enough, found him difficult to follow.

"The lumber company guys aren't your most sympathetic types," Ben said. "And when Quang says something they don't understand, I get the feeling no one's trying to cooperate. They screw him around a lot. They'll send him away with almost anything."

By June, Matthew was tired of being brought oversized nails, undersized staples and the wrong kind of glue. He told Ben he thought he was too forgiving of Quang. Ben insisted Matthew simply didn't understand. The issue became a contest of wills. When Quang did something well, Ben scored; when he didn't, it was a point for Matthew.

What was especially frustrating for Ben was the fact that even as Quang plodded along at work, he still managed to exert tremendous effort on his house. Instead of using his vacation time to go away, he spent a week tearing down the cinderblock garage that took up most of his back yard, but which sat empty because there was adequate parking on the street in front. The second week, he and Kim turned the yard into the garden area they'd wanted for planting Oriental vegetables. Ben struggled with his certainty that if he could only channel some of Quang's energy into the job, he could make him into something more than a laborer...a belief that for three years he hadn't been able to put into action.

In groping for possible reasons for the long impasse, we decided that perhaps Quang was as unhappy with his job as Matthew was

with his performance, yet stayed on out of some sense of obligation to
Ben. As he had done periodically in the past, Ben tried to make clear
that Quang was free to pursue whatever future he thought best for
him. Seizing on a discussion about a good friend, Chen, who went to
high school with Quang years ago in Vietnam and now was finishing
up an engineering degree in Indiana, Ben asked Quang if he didn't
want to go to college himself, at least to night school part-time. But
Quang, vague, only listed some of the projects he had left at home.
"Maybe when we pay more on the house," he said.

During that summer of 1978, we also began to feel that there was
some conflict over the issue of college at home. Kim wanted very
much for her family, especially Quang, to continue their educations.
"I work, I get very tired," she told me once. "But Minh and Lan, they
can learn, they can get good jobs, not like me." Although she was too
polite to extend this analogy to Quang since he was Ben's employee,
she would perk up noticeably when we talked about him taking a few
courses. "I want Quang go to school for engineer," she would say
wistfully, "like his friend."

And still Quang hedged. Wanting to counter Kim's uneasiness, we
suggested maybe *she* should take a course. She found that unthinkable. As they acquired some of the material things they wanted, Kim
retreated more and more into traditional ways of doing things.
Quang, the man, must have the education first. "Right now I don't
have time," she would say. "And someday I want another baby
...maybe when Tommy is four." So as Quang plodded along, though
Kim was doing remarkably well in her sewing work, she still regarded
herself as at the end of the line in a factory job, while bright futures
spread out for Quang and the others. If only they would go after
them. Ben suspected from what we heard that Kim attached far more
stigma to physical work than we did, and for that reason, too,
pressured Quang to move into white-collar work like his friends. But
Quang, oblivious to all of us, slowly went on his way, whether out of a
sense of duty or because of the financial security or because of
thoughts so different from ours that we couldn't begin to imagine
them. We had no idea.

Not until October 1978, was there a hint of change, of a new
confidence in Quang. That month the city of Crestville sent a notice
to Quang and his neighbors on either side that they would either have
to repair the sidewalk in front of their houses or be assessed to have
the city do it. The sidewalk was badly heaved by the roots of the big

old street trees. A year before Quang would have submissively paid the tax. Now he decided he knew enough about concrete work to pour the walk himself, at a fraction of the price the city wanted, if the neighbors would help. He had soon organized them into a work crew, bought the materials and was acting as supervisor one Saturday morning, overseeing the setting of forms, mixing and pouring of concrete, trowelling of the finished walk. Though Ben had suspected Quang must have some leadership abilities after his stint as a Vietnamese Navy oficer, this was the first time he had seen him in action.

That was to be only the beginning. Coupled with his new confidence was an assertiveness we had not seen before. While the sidewalk was torn up, he and the neighbor in the other half of his double house had hired Ben's plumber to run separate water lines in. Before, the whole building had been on one meter, so that the two of them had to split the bill without really knowing who used what.

Then the bills came. The plumber had charged Quang nearly $50 more than he had the American next door, though the distance from the main to the two sections of the house was roughly the same.

"He think we stupid because we have accent," Minh told us. "He think we don't know the difference."

For the first time ever, we saw Quang really upset. He hadn't expected to be cheated by a fellow worker he saw on the job at least once a week. He showed Ben the bill and asked him what to do. Ben told Quang to pay only what was fair and drafted a note explaining the situation, for Quang to send to the plumber. "It doesn't hurt to say you think he made a mistake," Ben told him. "That way the plumber can get out of it with honor, so you can speak to him again and nobody will be embarrassed."

"In my country," said Kim darkly, "somebody do this to you, you *no* speak to him again." But Quang sent the letter: he was ready to do things the American way, ready to put his anger to work. And the plumber soon adjusted the bill.

As quickly as it had surfaced, however, Quang's new aggressiveness seemed to subside. We were not to see it again until the middle of the winter, until February 1979.

Characteristically, several houses came up for closing just when the weather was at its worst, houses for which the foundations had been put in the fall before. Quang seemed to clean them at more of a snail's pace than ever, but Matthew, thoroughly discouraged, passed this off as his usual work speed: "If he went any slower, he'd be moving backwards. He's always that way." Unconvinced, Ben suspected a deliberate slowdown, and his suspicion was confirmed in early March, after Ben and Matthew had reviewed everyone for raises. Quang came in to complain about his salary.

"When I first come here," he told Ben, "I get pay more than my friends. Now they make more than me. So I don't work too hard now. When I clean the houses, I go too slow."

Ben had been through versions of his standard motivational speech several times before, but this time it had a telling effect. Quang would get no better job by sandbagging, Ben insisted. He would move up by doing only the best he possibly could, by showing he was capable. "Otherwise you can hang around forever and never be much further along than when you started. If you want more pay, do more work. It's that simple."

It was not that simple, of course. Quang's friends, for the most part, worked in factories where more work was, if anything, discouraged. Laborers were allowed to put out per hour what the union had negotiated as fair, nothing beyond that, lest management discover that more was indeed possible on a regular basis. Even Kim's job, where doing more piecework meant more pay, was slow and steady and repetitive, demanding no initiative. More could be done, but it was always more of the same.

Nevertheless, Quang seemed suddenly interested, after three years of apathy. Ben and Matthew's theory of leadership by example seemed now to have made its mark: the two of them worked consistently harder and longer and better than anyone they hired. Maybe, after all, that was how they got there.

"Kim, she have another baby in October," Quang told Ben. "I think about my future."

And Ben, far from being discouraged by Quang's dissatisfaction, was encouraged to see him showing some spunk.

As Tommy's birth had been two years before, now Kim's new pregnancy was a turning point of sorts for Quang. In the spring a friend of his came up from Baltimore to live with the family for a time—a bachelor named Hoan who had been having emotional difficulties. Alone, unhappy in the city, he came to Crestville to get a taste of stable family life—a compliment to Kim and Quang, we thought, that they should be considered so well-adjusted. While they waited for Hoan's factory job to come through, Quang asked if he could come to work temporarily for Ben. Matthew was away; Ben said yes, on the condition that Hoan—who had always lived among Vietnamese and spoke very little English—answer directly to Quang. During those two weeks, Quang used Hoan to demonstrate to Ben exactly what he could do. He gave Hoan orders and showed him how to do the work. As Ben and Matthew tried to do, he set a pace just a little faster than Hoan could maintain, though still slower than Ben would have liked. It was clear that Hoan was impressed enough to notice. "Hoan certainly thinks Quang is *macho*," he said in astonishment. At last Quang had shown that he was able to supervise. The question was: could he supervise Americans? The great debate began.

"American laborers will only go as fast as Quang does, and still take their coffee breaks besides," Matthew said. Ben disagreed. In late March, Quang's friend Chen received his engineering degree in Indiana and came east. Chen prided himself on being able to deal with Americans, almost to the point of being irritating. He made a great deal of the jobs he had taken to help support himself during college, while his sponsors—an elderly doctor and his wife—paid his tuition. Every conversation seemed punctuated by the references to how hard he had worked. One evening he told a joke he thought Ben would like, about a Vietnamese and a Westerner fishing together by the side of the river.

"I have only a few days off," the Westerner said. "Then I have to go back and work hard at my job."

"What for?" the Vietnamese asked.

"I'm trying to make enough money to buy my own business," said the Westerner.

"And then what?" asked the Vietnamese.

"Put away enough for retirement."

"And then?"

"Maybe do some fishing," the Westerner said.

To which the Vietnamese replied, with a puzzled look on his face, "But you are fishing *now*."

Everyone laughed, especially Chen himself, but for Ben the joke brought home the point of Chen's incessant and none-too-subtle references to work. Chen—and apparently Quang, too, now—had come to understand the great emphasis Americans place on hard work and wanted to demonstrate that they now shared it. With that sort of understanding, Ben argued to Matthew, it was reasonable to suppose Quang would now work just that much harder if he were made a supervisor.

In mid-April the debate was finally put to a stop by the course of events. Ben bought several lots in a lake community about 40 minutes away. He hired two new laborers and started talking about summer help. The company had reached the point where he needed someone to be in charge of the labor pool, who could oversee the work and send laborers where they were needed from day to day. Quang had been doing the job for nearly four years. He knew exactly what needed to be done to prepare the houses for closing. He was promoted to foreman of the labor pool.

Quang soon appeared to be outperforming even Ben's most optimistic projections. His Step n' Fetchit stance had almost disappeared. He was capable, it seemed, of firmness, even yelling and swearing when the occasion called for it, though Ben and Matthew found his Vietnamese-tinged curses more amusing than intimidating. "The laborers listen to him," Matthew said grudgingly. "I don't know how he does it, but they do listen."

Only once was there trouble. A new laborer asked if insulation was to be installed the next day. Quang said he didn't think so. When the work schedule for the following day was changed to include insulating after all, the laborer flatly refused to do it. "I wore short sleeves because you said we weren't going to insulate," the laborer told Quang. "I'd get that picky fiberglass all over me." He would put in insulation only in long sleeves.

Quang told Ben about the incident, and Ben reacted angrily. "Why didn't you fire him on the spot? You can't have guys working for you refusing to do the work." The laborer was dismissed...but more importantly, Quang realized that he had not only supervisory duties, but powers as well. Secure in the knowledge that he could hire and fire, he had no more difficulties maintaining his authority.

The new job brought with it not only a hike in pay, but a big increase in prestige as well. Quang learned the management game as quickly as he had once learned the labor work slowly. Seeing that Ben would never give instructions to the workers on the site, but only to Matthew, and that Matthew would talk only to the foremen of the crews, Quang did his best to make his new position known. "You need a house cleaned up," he said one day to Craig, "You come to me."

Soon Quang, along with Craig and Matthew, was one of the men who attended weekly administrative sessions with Ben to plan the upcoming work. Matthew, once Quang's severest critic, now rated him among the top three or four men who, during the predicted upcoming recession, he would want to keep.

One day in the middle of the summer Quang was guiding a hulking bulldozer operator, Joe, as he pushed backfill in toward the foundation, motioning him when to add more dirt, when to stop, working with some degree of concentration.

"You almost finished?" Matthew called to Joe when he was unable to attract Quang's attention. Joe motioned to Quang.

"I will be as soon as Old Grouchy here lets me," he said.

"From smiling when he flunked his driving test to being called Old Grouchy by a dozer operator who considers himself the essence of macho...now *that's* coming a long way," Ben decided. What this new attitude will do to his blood pressure in years to come and whether it will give him ulcers, we don't know. But it seemed to be assuring him of at least temporary survival in the American rat race...and that looked to us like progress.

Not everything had changed. Kim, with all her graciousness, was the well-bred Vietnamese lady more than ever. Visiting at their house one night shortly after we heard about her pregnancy, we asked her how she felt. And she, looking pale and drawn as if she hadn't slept for weeks, smiled wanly and replied, "I feel fine, thank you." To which Minh, who had just walked into the room, waved her hands in mock disgust and said, "She sick every day." It turned out she was having trouble with her allergies more than with morning sickness. Since her doctor doesn't want her taking antihistamines while she's pregnant, she spends many nights awake, unable to breathe.

When the children asked why the two of them told different stories, Ben said it was because Kim grew up in Vietnam and would never want to answer with bad news...while Minh, growing up here, would not think it matters so much. Even if we knew Kim all our lives, we would never be able to read her moods. She signaled them to us in a code she learned before she came here, as closed to us as her language. We did the best we could. But mostly things resolved themselves. In early summer, Kim's cousin, Fon, called Ben while he was visiting. It was the first we'd heard from him in more than three years. He apologized for giving Ben so much trouble while he lived here and said he had a good job now and was sorry.

"Uh-oh," I said, remembering Fon's apologies. "I wonder what he *really* wants."

It turned out he wanted nothing. He visited and then left, to return to his home in Delaware. We agreed that we must have misjudged him. Fon, too, had apparently made his peace.

And on Tommy's third birthday in May 1979, Kim invited us to dinner, though she said Tommy was too old now for big parties and she, pregnant, was too tired to entertain all the friends. We sat around after the meal listening to Quang and Chen and Hoan talk about Vietnam as they had known it before.

"In my country," Quang said, "you work, you don't work, life is the same unless you are very rich. In this country, if you work hard you can live better. If you don't work, you have nothing."

A long sigh. Four years before he had brought rock tapes instead of clothes, and looked at us with hungry eyes, yearning for American goods. No more. Far from believing that American wealth was available but mysteriously elusive, the family had developed the basis for facing their future realistically. In America, they themselves, not outside benefactors, would power their lives.

EPILOGUE

Human rights go beyond speeches. We learned that doing something meant putting up with the day-to-day frustrations of helping people whose idea of help was often quite different from ours. We wished at the time we'd had some support, and we didn't—and it's only in retrospect that we see why.

When the refugees arrived here in 1975, the United States was in the process of leaving Vietnam, with great relief but also with a certain amount of embarrassment. We had never gone home in defeat before: the refugees would be our visible reminder. At the same time, unemployment here was high. There was a great outcry for existing jobs to go to Americans, not to 125,000 foreigners—this though the United States is a nation of foreigners and though only about 25,000 of the refugees would actually be entering the job market. Despite the normally compassionate nature of the American people, the mood was ugly. The anti-war, human rights activists of the early 70's had quietly gone underground. The refugees couldn't have come to a more hostile environment. As a practical matter, it became national policy to shotgun them throughout the country, to keep them from becoming a noticeable blight.

Even then, the transition was not always pretty. In some places, feeling against the refugees was high enough that there was concern for their physical safety. Competition for fishing waters in some southern communities was to lead to long-lasting outbursts of racial violence. As this is written in the spring of 1981, the Vietnamese shrimpers in Texas are still involved in litigation against the Ku Klux Klan. No wonder, then, that after a flurry of media activity over the resettlement camps and sponsorship program, there was a great, healing silence in 1975. The refugees, in any great numbers that required national concern, seemed not to exist.

And maybe for most of the country the silence *was* healing. But for us, the refugees and their sponsors, particularly those of us who were located away from large urban centers, it was difficult indeed. Two cultures do not mesh without snags. And yet no one (was it possible?) seemed to know what we were in for. The soothing government pamphlets that might have appeared to ease us over the bumps never materialized. The young couple we had contact with at Catholic Charities in Baltimore had been given no more training than we had...and though they meant well and certainly worked hard, what could they tell us? Where were the television interviews with settled Vietnamese-Americans (surely there *were* some?) detailing what the adjustment had been like for them? When we fell into conflict with Kim and Quang, what else were we to think but that our problems were unique? Neither the media or the government or other sponsors in the community had given any indication otherwise. How were we to know that there were people not three miles away going through the same thing...and that, like us, they felt too guilty to talk about it? By the time we found out, many of the sponsor relationships had disintegrated. Except for Kim's pregnancy, ours might have too.

In many ways the difficulties faced by the church congregations sponsoring refugees were even worse. Certainly they were more complex. As individuals we knew from the outset that our finances and our strengths were not inexhaustible, and we were forced to spell out (with mixed success) the limitations we intended to impose on our charity. Most church congregations felt no such restraints. Going in, when feeling was high, the tendency was to want to make the grand gesture—to provide almost complete financial support "at least until he speaks enough English to get a good job," "at least until they can afford a car," "at least until they have enough money saved." The problem with such vague "at leasts" was that they were so open-ended. The refugees, understandably, saw them as indefinite, and the congregations did too, until the daily frustrations of running errands and paying bills made it seem suddenly desirable to fit them into a time frame. The few active workers had grown weary; the financial outlays which had seemed so reasonable during the drama of the spring appeared less so by winter when the refugees had evolved into people rather than symbols of oppressed humanity. Limits were set, timetables mentioned...and when that happened, the refugees understandably felt betrayed.

To O and Nga, the family which eventually fled from Crestville to Baltimore, the realization that O would have to do something even if it meant taking a blue-collar job must have come as a terrible shock. By subsidizing his rent on the old parsonage, by providing free care for his child, by cushioning every contact he made, the congregation did everything to protect him from the realities of life here and nothing to introduce him to them. Their decision to impose conditions, when no provision had been made at the outset for the various steps in his move to independence, must have seemed to him capricious as well as cruel.

By the spring of 1976, most of the refugees in Crestville and other small communities around the country had made just enough money to leave if they wanted to. Leave they did. They went to Baltimore, to Washington, to Los Angeles...and they went with stories of the Americans who had cheated them, mistreated them, misled them. Life here had not been what they expected. And they left behind them sponsors—often whole church congregations—who thought that they too had been misinterpreted, misunderstood, taken advantage of. Could the bitterness have been avoided if someone had warned the participants in advance? I think so. A little guidance, a little ongoing publicity about the problems (not just the one-a-year progress reports in big newspapers like the Washington Post) might have helped.

This is not to say that the migration toward the cities could have been avoided, or should have been. Under the best of circumstances, depriving the refugees of the support of their peers by scattering them across the country was cruel. Most of the refugees arrived penniless. They were unable to travel independently because of their financial straits during those first months, and so were virtually at the mercy of the American sponsors they had been sent to throughout the nation. When those sponsors were church congregations with varying ideas of what to do, how much support to give, the problem was often insurmountable. But what if they had known in advance what their sponsors would probably expect from them? What if the sponsors had known, from the silent experts, what snags to anticipate? Would the breaks have been such angry ones? I think not. Alas, human rights (human feelings?) in 1975 and '76 took second place to our national need to forget. That first year was an avoidable disaster.

As everyone knows today, it didn't make any difference in the long run. The success of the Vietnamese in this country has been phenomenal. They have shown themselves to be a proud, independent people able to regroup under extremely trying conditions. After a brief period of readjustment, they showed without question that our way of life suited them. Department of Health, Education and Welfare statistics in mid-1979 indicated that 94 percent of all heads of households among the 1975 refugees were employed. Four years after their arrival, Kim and Quang owned a house and two cars. What has happened in the two years since this journal ended is no less revealing.

Kim's second son, Bobby, was born in October 1979, and was soon placed in day care with Tommy so Kim could continue to work. By 1980, the family had enough saved to buy a second, more modern house. They kept the first one as a rental property. And now they are on the brink of another great change—starting their own home improvement business in California.

Many things have precipitated this move. When Lan graduated from high school in 1979, she went to California to college, so she could be near a boyfriend who had moved west with his family. Last summer they were married. During the trip out for the wedding, Quang was besieged with questions from Vietnamese friends about having work done on their houses. The large Vietnamese community near Los Angeles was still distrustful of American contractors; there weren't any Vietnamese ones. Since, at the time, Lan and her new husband hoped to return to Crestville in a year or so, after they had earned enough money for a down payment on a house, Quang gave the matter no further thought. But then Lan became pregnant and quit work, and the prospect of a house in Maryland drew dimmer. The large manufacturing plant here where Lan's husband hoped to work was hit hard by the depressed economy; there were extensive layoffs but no hiring. By the time Lan's baby was born, it appeared they would be in California indefinitely.

At the same time, Kim's allergies had grown steadily worse. The new house, away from the park, was expected to bring her some relief, but it didn't. Where once a game of tennis or other exercise would clear her head, now even medication doesn't help much. She spends her summers, particularly, unable to breathe freely or sleep well.

And now, in June, word has just arrived that Kim's father has escaped from Vietnam to Malaysia, an event the family has been anticipating for more than four years. When he comes to the United States, they feel, he will be more comfortable in a warm climate, among other Vietnamese. Minh, a college sophomore, will transfer from the University of Maryland to one of the California schools. They will all be together again.

So Quang has his two houses for sale, and in spite of high interest rates, he already has a buyer for the rental property. The new house should go soon too for a tidy profit, because he spent the winter finishing the basement into a family room. When he leaves, he'll take his carpentry and business skills with him, and about $50,000 in cash. In many respects Quang isn't all that atypical of the first wave of refugees. In just six years, he's done better under the American system than many Americans ever do.

If there's a lesson to be learned from all this, especially now that it appears the problem of refugees from vastly different cultures may be with us for some time, it is not that we must all sympathize and perhaps lend some of our old clothes and good advice to the cause (there was too much of that the first time), but that we might try to be aware that two cultures don't mesh without conflict. And while the eventual outcome may not be affected, the initial adjustment can certainly be cushioned by solid information and moral support. We might, in other words, become a bit more sophisticated about the overview.

My impression is that this is happening only partially. On the positive side, Catholic Charities in Baltimore is no longer sending out subsidy money in one lump sum, $300 per person, as it did in 1975. By 1979, refugees and their sponsors had to ask for the money for specific purposes and back their requests with receipts. This, I think, was good. Too often the refugees who received the 1975 subsidies placed them in savings and then regarded them as nonexistent, while continuing to live on the charity, both public and private, that the subsidies were intended to make unnecessary. To the best of my knowledge, none of the refugees in Crestville ever reported subsidy monies as income to the welfare authorities. In almost every case, the subsidies collected interest for some years and then were used—as Kim and Quang's were—for house down payments, cars or other comparative luxuries. This would not have been so objectionable if the subsidies had been distributed universally, as outright grants to all the refugees. But they weren't, and the idea was always to help them with initial expenses.

Under the new system, Catholic Charities is able to supply more money to families that need it, less to those that don't. When Kim's uncle arrived as one of the boat people late in 1979, he was able to secure subsidy funds for his first month's rent, security deposit, and initial filling of his heating oil tank—all, obviously, genuine needs for someone trying to get settled. Then, because he was working at a steady job, he got no more, though funds were available for unforeseen expenses. Far more than in 1975, the monies were being distributed so that they didn't hinder the overall objective of financial self-sufficiency for the refugees.

Not all the refugee services are using the government subsidies this way. Some earmark them for administrative expenses and never dole them out to the refugees at all. I think this is wrong. Where sponsorships do not work out, the refugees are at a special disadvantage if they have no source of lump-sum income at the moment when they may have to strike out on their own. It would seem desirable to have the subsidies universally available in hardship cases, and in such a way that the refugees could ask for them directly, not necessarily through sponsors. At the Indochina Center in Baltimore, for example, some of the staff speak Vietnamese. What would be wrong with providing their phone number to incoming refugees, so that they could call it in an emergency without help from sponsors, even if they were located elsewhere in the state?

Another disturbing aspect of refugee service policy by late 1979 was that it seemed to have shifted so as to make it virtually impossible for individuals to become sponsors. The theory was that only churches, with their collective manpower and financial strength, had the resources to cope with the problems involved. While some of the refugee organizations denied that this was the official position, we knew several individuals who tried to sponsor families, only to meet in every case with insurmountable administrative hurdles. This, I thought, was unwise. Among the people we knew who offered themselves unsuccessfully as sponsors were Chris and Mike Flowers, mentioned earlier in this account for their efforts to help Van and Trinh. Though those efforts were disappointing—perhaps *because* they were—Chris and Mike were especially well suited to understand the problems that would be likely to arise. They were told by the refugee service to get their church involved. But the church, disillusioned by Van and Trinh, was not interested. As longtime residents of the community, owners of a business, active both in church and civic affairs, Chris and Mike were in an excellent position themselves to locate jobs, housing, medical care and other services. One of the great problems that has always existed with church sponsorships is the lack of enough concerned *individuals* to work with the refugees over a long period of time on a one-to-one basis. Many churches, in fact, have always been concerned primarily with attracting converts, with bitter consequences for the refugees otherwise.

"After one year," Quang told us recently of a family that had been sponsored by a church in Crestville, "our friends not go to church every Sunday. Then they see sponsors in grocery store, but nobody say hi."

Or in another case, where the church administration changed shortly after a refugee family arrived: "The new pastor come, nobody help them anymore." With concerned individuals taking the responsibility in the first place, this is unlikely to happen.

This is not to say that many churches have not done an excellent job with their refugees over the years. Some have guided not one but large numbers of refugee groups to independence, bringing in new families as soon as the previous ones were settled. In this way, they have provided both American help and much-needed Vietnamese contacts to the newcomers during the first crucial days.

Typically, these successful churches have had a core group of individuals who have dealt closely with the refugees while drawing backup from the rest of the congregation. This is not so different from what a dedicated individual family can do, drawing support from the secular community. The difficulty, of course, is that it is more time-consuming to screen individual applicants. It's easier, and politically safer, for the voluntary agencies to give the okay to a church.

One of the staff members we know at Catholic Charities says her biggest problem is finding sponsors who won't overprotect their families. The successful churches have avoided overprotection because the few individuals directly responsible for the refugees have been sensitive to it. Where the core leadership has been less stable, it has been all too easy to recruit errand-runners or service-providers long after the need for them has waned, simply to avoid conflict with refugees who may be virtual strangers to the people trying to help them. When the novelty wears off, it is equally easy to withdraw support too suddenly and too totally. It *is* exhausting to run errands incessantly, but it is something that has to be done (indeed, *should* be done) only for a short time. An individual family, properly screened and properly prepared, has less opportunity to overprotect, more to understand the nuances of the relationship that only close contact can reveal. At the very worst, many individual families are as willing and as well-qualified to act as sponsors as churches. I think it's unfair to exclude them on the charge that they are not.

131

Still, this seems to me less disturbing than the fact that neither sponsors nor refugees are receiving much more guidance than they were in 1975, although since about 1977 a great deal of helpful material has been available for both. In the spring of 1979, we watched one local church take on a semi-literate boat family and soon repeat virtually every mistake that could have been predicted from the experience of four years before. As had been done in the past, the family was situated in a house for which the church paid rent and utilities. No arrangements were made for them to eventually take over expenses. The church also decided that, since the man of the family had previously been a fisherman, the best policy would be to let him go to school at first, then look for work when he knew more English. This decision was made in spite of the fact that work was available for him—as a laborer, to be sure, but *work*—and that language classes could be arranged to suit his schedule. Six months later, a weary congregation was still unwillingly supporting the family, with a little help from welfare. The parishioners were bitterly disappointed in the family's slow progress in English, though what they had expected from semi-literates no one seemed to know. The family, also desperately unhappy, could not leave because they simply didn't have the money to move. And worse, the frustrations were being taken out in small cruelties. When a member of the Vietnamese family called the woman in charge of medical care, saying she needed to be taken to a doctor, the parishioner refused. "I am sick, too," she said. "I can't help you." Ultimately the family turned to Kim and Quang to see them through the emergency. Without a car, without money for cabfare, without the know-how to call a doctor or take a bus, they had yet to develop a shred of the independence they so sorely needed.

This seemed to me especially lamentable because part of the reason these problems developed was that the people most in need of the information that was available simply hadn't gotten it. By 1979, things had changed. Catholic Charities was sending out a whole packet of introductory government materials on how to deal with and settle refugees. Today, they send personal representatives to talk to interested groups beforehand and anticipate some of the problems. The Lutheran refugee service group in Baltimore has a film available to be shown to such groups beforehand. Unfortunately, the people who get the material aren't always the ones who end up doing the work later. There's still quite a gap between the refugee services and the committee members who might take over several months into the sponsorship.

Nor is all the material coming out awfully realistic. Consider a bilingual pamphlet called "A Guide to Two Cultures," which attempts to introduce the refugee to his American sponsor and vice versa. While much of the information is invaluable (the discussion of the Vietnamese inability to say no, for example), the section on Vietnamese entertaining habits is baffling. The Vietnamese will be reluctant to entertain you in their homes at first, the pamphlet says; they may be more inclined to take you to a restaurant. It was at least a year before Kim and Quang could have considered going to a restaurant *themselves*, much less taking us. When we asked them whether this practice was common in Vietnam, they told us it was limited to the very rich families in the cities. Kim's family, well-to-do government officials, normally entertained at home.

The danger of these federally-sanctioned half-truths, I think, is that they confound an already bewildering situation for everyone. When misunderstandings occur, what is wanted is realistic advice, not more confusion, information that is as accurate and as broad-based as possible. While some of the 1975 refugees were from the very richest Saigon families, not all of them were, and the boat people who came later tended to be less educated, less sophisticated still. Pity the poor church members who wait for their refugee family—illiterate fishermen, unemployed—to take them out to dinner at a restaurant!

If realistic information can be gotten out at the beginning of a program, when refugees from an unfamiliar culture first arrive, rather than two or more years later, that too would be invaluable. Today several hundred thousand Indochinese have settled throughout the United States, and can provide concrete help to newcomers even in the smallest towns, just as Kim and Quang helped the illiterate fisherman when his sponsorship floundered. So the abundance of government information, helpful as it is, is in no way as important as it would have been in 1975 and 1976 when the refugees had only each other to talk to, when misinformation and bitterness were rife. Is it unrealistic to expect accurate information to be put out *en masse* during the first few months of another potential refugee influx? I think not. Commercial presses have been known to turn out whole books within weeks of disasters, assassinations and the like. Surely this technique could be adapted to more humane ends.

This is not to suggest that a massive public information effort could forestall all potential problems. When Kim's uncle and his family arrived in 1979, we were surprised to find that Kim and Quang had many of the same problems with the family during their first year that we had had earlier. The uncle complained bitterly about his expenses, especially his fuel bills, about which he had been forewarned. (His landlord, in fact, began to feel so guilty because of his complaining that he put in half a tank of oil at his own expense.) As soon as the uncle began to save money, he hooked up to cable TV and paid extra for the Home Box Office option. He and Quang had a bitter fight about this. Home Box Office could wait until later, Quang said. Cable alone gave him a wide selection of channels. He didn't need an extra monthly bill just for a few movies. The uncle ignored him. He wanted Home Box Office *now*. Nor could he understand why he couldn't buy a house when Quang had one, or a new car, and so on.

"I tell him you work, you save money, then you buy," Quang told us. "But he no understand." The uncle believed that Quang had been given a large sum of subsidy money that he wasn't getting and, in part, this was true. He also thought he was entitled to something extra because he had fought on the American side in Vietnam and spent two years in jail afterwards as a result. He was certain there was some information—or more particularly, some money—we weren't telling him about.

And so we went through the year of disappointment all over again, though Kim and Quang bore the brunt of it. Even among relatives who shared a language and a culture, appearances were deceiving. The uncle didn't believe Quang's story that he got *all that* through sheer hard work. But time passed and, sure enough, the uncle began to see it could be done. In many ways, adjustment is a process. There is only so much anyone can do beyond letting it take its course.

Even six years later, there remain some Indochinese who still do not understand that the objective of the sponsorship program is independence. A Catholic Charities staff member told me recently of a man who arrived in Baltimore this winter from California. "He'd been here since 1975 and he wanted another sponsor," she said. "He didn't understand that once you move, you're on your own." I suspect that, no matter what refinements in the program are made, there will always be a little of that.

The important thing is that, as new refugee groups come in, the lessons of the past not be repeated. Are they? The recent wave of Cuban refugees, culturally and linguistically much closer to us than the Indochinese were, have been having their share of problems under the sponsor system these past few years. What about the Ethiopians who are coming in now? They are black, but I've been told they relate, so far, neither to the black community nor to the white, only to each other. How much more difficult will it be for them?

But without a summary of past lessons from some authoritative source—the federal government, the refugee services who've been through it before—it may be harder still. In 1975 there was no way except by harsh experience for either sponsors or refugees to find out what they were in for. It would have been reassuring to know in advance that human rights is not so much the grand gesture of providing a year's free rent as small, draining efforts like picking up grammar books in 90 degree heat, finding an obstetrician, dealing with an abusive landlord. Or explaining that even in a blistery Maryland winter, a different heavy jacket is not required for each day of the week. It is refusing to offer a ride so that a refugee will have to learn to use the bus. And being thought uncharitable as a result.

For the refugees, it is important to know at the outset that America sometimes begins in tenement quarters, even if rumor has always whispered of opulence, of cars, of houses with eight or nine rooms. It is important to know that sympathetic Americans love to speak of what should be done, but will rarely do it for you, and often won't even tell you how to do it yourself. It is important to be prepared for the mechanic who equates broken English with stupidity and will try to take advantage. It is no fun. The people who get involved have a right to know this. The argument can be made that the first time no one knew what to predict (though I don't believe it). Now we do.